Feed Your Need

Discover the simple food, hormone and motivation facts that really make a difference. This will work.

Corinne Peachment

MARPEL

Published in 2000 by

MARPEL

P. O. Box 8478
Austin, Texas
U.S.A. 78713-8478

The Library of Congress has catalogued this edition as:

Peachment, Corinne. 1956 -
Feed Your Need: Discover the simple food hormone and motivation facts
that really make a difference. – 1st ed.
ISBN 0-9673462-0-7
1. Nutrition.   2. Title   I. Peachment, Corinne
612.3-dc20   99-74743

Disclaimer
Although information in this book is based on the author's
extensive clinical and hospital based experience, it is not intended
to substitute for the advice of a physician. Discuss any dietary or
exercise changes with your holistic health practitioner.
Professional supervision is essential for those taking medication
and/or suffering from an acute or chronic illness.

Editor: Marc Rose

Cover Design: George Foster

Book Design: Terry Sherrell

Printed in U.S.A.

About the Author

Corinne Peachment holds five degrees, including a Science degree from Queen's University, Canada and a Masters degree from Australia. Her postgraduate food and hormone related research earned Dean's honors. In 1991 she was appointed as the Clinical Educator for the Division of Medicine at St. George Hospital in Sydney, Australia. Further work involved eight years as a diabetes and weight specialist in several hospitals, including a University of Toronto affiliated teaching hospital.

She has worked closely with endocrinologists from South Africa and The Middle East and has been an invited speaker at international medical conferences in New Zealand, Australia and Canada. Her outstanding efforts in health education won a $5,000 award of excellence from the Australian division of Boerhinger Mannheim. She lives in Texas.

Thank you to:

Jack Canfield,
for describing possibilities &

Maya Angelou
Dr. Richard K. Bernstein
Dr. Vincent Bellonzi
Dr. Herbert Benson
Dr. Joan Borysenko
Dr. John Bradshaw
Les Brown
Dr. Leo Buscalia
Dr. Richard Carlson
David Chilton
Dr. Robin Cook
Dr. Mary Dan Eades
Dr. Micheal Eades
Brian Edwards
Dr. Joel Goodman
Thich Nhat Hanh
Mark Victor Hansen
Dr. Louise Hay
Margie Ingram

Dr. John Kabat-Zinn
Dr. Paul Kahl
Micheline Lannoy
Dr. John R. Lee
Marc Macaulay
Dr. S. Mallette-Edwards
Susan Muir
Dr. Christiane Northrup
Chris Peachment
Dr. Scott Peck
Dr. Judith Reichman
Marc Rose
Tom & Marilyn Ross
David Roth
Dr. Robert Schuller
Dr. Barry Sears
Dr. Martin Seligman
Gloria Steinem
Dr. Dennis Waitley

... the giant shoulders on which to stand.

Contents

Part I — Discover Food

Part II — Plan to Win

Preface

The most sensible health advice is of little use if it is too complicated to understand. Busy people, whether homemakers or rocket scientists, want brief and practical answers. The purpose of this book is to present some simple answers to the complex topic of food, hormones and motivation. Yet simplicity is not meant to encourage black or white thinking. Truth is often a complicated paradox. As Albert Einstein once said, "everything should be made as simple as possible, but not simpler." And above all, may you play the food game with a spirit of joy, curiosity and action, for this is love and love is what we are.

Corinne Peachment

Part I

Discover Food

1.

Welcome New Beliefs

*Conventional wisdom is an odd
expression because 9 times out of 10, if
it's conventional, it's not wisdom.*

Herb Kelleher,
CEO Southwest Airlines

Your Thoughts

This book can turn your life around. I know
because I've seen it happen. As I begin writing these
words I am employed in a major city teaching
hospital where my close co-workers include an

anorexic dietitian, a depressed psychologist and a chronically ill physician. This situation is far from uncommon and there is much truth to the idea of the wounded healer. Health professionals often enter their field of work in search of personal answers that may never be found.

New discoveries rarely come from the so-called "experts" but from what author Dr. Maxwell Maltz refers to as "inperts." Einstein, for example, was a mathematician yet his findings altered the world of physics. Madame Curie contributed to medical science, yet she was not a physician.

Most doctors and dietitians know little about the information you have in your hand. Yet there are a growing number of scientists and physicians who support the ideas presented in this book. These include top nutritionists and psychologists from Harvard University and the University of Toronto.

The discovery of life changing ideas can be painfully slow. Over the past 30 years I have found only a few remarkable books that really made a difference in my life. None of these appeared during the nine years I spent at university. They were discovered by listening to people who were leading incredibly healthy and productive lives.

While I value education, too much conventional schooling can prevent us from discovering our true potential. As Gloria Steinem once said "a little disrespect for formal education can be useful, since it so often disrespects us." The hypnosis of formal schooling can lead us down a conforming road of narrow vision.

This book will guide you to the road of possibilities. I promise that it can improve and lengthen your life. My promise, however, is based on the condition that you at least follow the suggestions for a minimum of six weeks. Nothing useful happens without action. The sum of many small actions determines our outcomes.

Any wise reader will be skeptical of my promise. I recently listened to a respected author say, "be wary of self-help books that promise miracle cures." Historically, I was in complete agreement. In the past I would not have believed that slight alterations in food intake could cause such enormous changes in health and energy. Yet I now know that food is powerful medicine. The mix, timing and amount of food consumed alters both our immediate level of alertness and the quality of our lives.

Unfortunately, enjoying great health rewards means beginning with an open mind and a willingness to truly question current food beliefs. Experience has shown that *this is the greatest stumbling block for most people.* Reading a few words is easy, but getting rid of deeply ingrained past conditioning requires a different approach.

If you are serious about improving the quality of your life, then consider one of author Jack Canfield's sayings:

If you keep believing what you've been believing, you will keep achieving what you've been achieving.

What beliefs do you hold about food? For example, do you think that carrots are "good" and ice cream is "bad?" Whatever your beliefs, do you have clear evidence to support them? Or is your evidence based on advertising, your parents, friends, newspapers, television, emotionalism or even ill-informed health professionals? If so, then this book will provide you with some current scientific facts. These facts comes from the world's best, peer-reviewed medical journals, not some health store pamphlet, advertising flyer or fashion magazine.

The second stumbling block to great health is a refusal to examine and act on the details. For example, I recently attended a medical conference where one of the lecturers spoke about a variety of different diet books. The presenter, who happened to be a dietitian and personal friend, was ill-prepared. She later admitted to having read only a couple of pages of each book. Even specialized health professionals cannot be depended on to keep up to date on the details of new research.

Results are in the details

It is also important that you be the judge. Look at the results you are achieving. The true test of any health advice is how well you feel and what your measured medical tests reveal. These measures, such as blood pressure, insulin levels and triglycerides are excellent predictors of your current and future health.

If your present food beliefs and habits do not keep you feeling physically and mentally alert and free from pain and illness, then it's time to change. I promise that you can improve the quality of your life. Simply begin. Take the first small step and keep moving forwards. Don't let anything or anyone discourage you from getting the results you desire.

Habits are Health

These steps to great health need not be painful or filled with unrealistic discipline. The "no-pain, no-gain" philosophy of well-being is not true. You do not need to spend hours a day engaged in strenuous exercise. While moderate activity and good *daily habits* are essential, strict deprivation and emotional pain are not. In fact, when we try too hard or hold on too tightly, we miss the great rewards of this bountiful life.

Good habits also allow for regular relaxation and flexibility, especially during special occasions. No one benefits from psychologically beating themselves up over imperfections. Food is friend, not foe, and you are always as close as your next meal to getting back on track. Follow reasonable daily habits, stray when necessary, and free yourself to improve one day at a time. Adopt a "play the game" attitude and you will gain peace of mind and better health.

Any anxiety or guilt from perceived failure only contributes to health problems. Successful people see failure as just a delay in results. Yet chronic diet failure usually goes hand in hand with programs based solely on calorie or choice restriction. The new and exciting truth about food has less to do with calories and more to do with hormones. As biochemist Dr. Barry Sears says, "we are in the midst of a paradigm shift from caloric thinking to hormonal thinking."

This book will teach you how to enjoy food, eliminate cravings and feel consistently alert. It will help you live longer and reverse or prevent a wide variety of diseases. Athletes also benefit, as proven by Olympic gold medalists, elite basketball players, track and field stars, national football players and others.

This state of health is more than simple freedom from pain and illness. It is vitality, not merely survival. Or, as Dr. Scott Peck writes "health is not so much the absence of disease as the presence of an optimal healing system." This optimal healing system involves a balance of biochemical, physical, emotional, social, occupational and spiritual factors.

The foundation for physical well-being is based on the hormonal science of nutrition, not on emotionalism. Unfortunately, some people believe they are healthy, but are unaware of better possibilities.

Take a moment to ask yourself:

1) Are my food habits consistently helping me to feel alert, energetic and emotionally stable?

2) Are my food habits helping me to stay within the normal range for standard medical tests and am I free of pain or other symptoms of illness?

3) Are my food habits helping me to maintain a healthy amount of body fat and can I build muscle if I choose to exercise?

If you answered yes to all these questions, then your current way of eating is right for you. Keep eating what you've been eating! If you answered no to any of these questions then read on.

Education is Repetition

You don't need to be a science or math whiz to benefit from this book. Merely taking action on the key points in chapters eight and nine will create positive results. On the other hand, you will gain the most by reading each chapter more than once. Small details create success. One exposure rarely internalizes a message or alters habits. Education is repetition. Education is repetition. Once you understand how different foods affect hormones, blood sugar, fat storage, immunity and even emotions, you will realize the importance of food as medicine.

Knowing what to do is the first step, but knowing how to stay motivated is another hurdle. Understanding the psychological factors that surround food intake is just as important as knowing what to eat. But like millions of others, you *can* develop lifelong healthy habits. Chapter nine will provide some simple but powerful tips on this topic.

It may also help you to know that this book is the result of twenty years experience in health education. Dozens of topics have been explored, including meditation, acupuncture, herbs, humor, exercise, stress reduction, chiropractic, conventional drug therapy and much more. Of course many of these approaches are valuable and total health involves several factors. Yet food intake plays a major role in determining your health and longevity.

Paradoxically, it is wise to avoid obsessing over our personal well-being. For as Benjamin Franklin said, "Nothing is more fatal to health than an over care of it." The best outcome from this book is to eventually help the reader think less about food and more about living.

Joy of Change

There is solid evidence to support the guidelines presented in this book. Yet it often takes over ten years for newly-published scientific research to influence popular opinion. Why is progress so slow? One reason is that food habits have cultural and social significance that stubbornly resists change. And these belief systems, which are also held by health professionals, are embedded deeply in our subconscious mind.

For example, most doctors initially laughed at the idea of home blood glucose meters, yet they are now used almost worldwide in diabetes care. History has shown that ill-informed critics, even so called "experts" will fight tooth and nail to resist change. Yet given enough time and evidence, popular opinion does shift.

I know how stubborn others can be because I was one of them. As a Clinical Nurse Specialist in diabetes, I read journals, attended conferences and published papers, yet my food beliefs stayed the same. Part of me, however, knew that something about our approach had to be wrong. Conventional dietary advice was not working. My patients were lethargic, overweight and depressed, while their blood results remained hazardous.

I often wondered how so many patients, who were trying their best to follow our suggestions, still felt miserable. This problem was and is not solely due to laziness or lack of discipline. My patients, along with many others, had been given the wrong advice.

After years of searching and with much help, I finally came across a far superior approach that starkly contradicts conventional dietary wisdom. Now I continuously marvel at the renewed vitality of my patients. Just begin and know that beginning is really half finished. You will soon be achieving your goals. Continued motivation will also flow naturally when you read, reread and act on the information in chapter nine. *This chapter will be critically important for improving your outcomes.* Please read it.

2.

Know Your Food

*Theories, no matter how pertinent, cannot
eradicate the existence of facts.*

Jean Charcot

Hidden Contents

In addition to water, most food contains some
combination of protein, fat or carbohydrate. These
three food parts are called macronutrients, and scientists can predict how much of each macronutrient is contained in different foods. The mix and
timing of macronutrients you consume has both
immediate and long-term affects on your physical
and mental health.

Unfortunately, most people have no idea how
much protein, fat or carbohydrate they are eating.
For example, did you know that one plain bagel

contains more glucose (sugar) generating carbohydrate than three chocolate wafer-style candy bars? Similarly, your body turns one cup of baked beans into more blood glucose than five typical soft centered chocolate bars. Even those who are aware of what they are eating, typically focus on fat content. They rarely look at the protein and carbohydrate numbers. Yet it is the balance of *all three* macronutrients that is important.

This lack of knowledge is a little like trying to build a house while blindfolded. If you can't see the bricks, glass and steel needed to construct your home then it is impossible to build a sound structure. Similarly, if you are unaware of the amount of protein, fat or carbohydrate you are eating, then it is impossible to make the most of your mind and body.

Are You Building a Sound Structure?

Fortunately, this does not mean having to weigh, measure or become obsessed with every gram of food. Just a little understanding will enable you to eyeball different foods and quickly make appropriate choices. It is easy to choose from a wide variety of meals and snacks. Eating the foods you prefer and enjoy makes it simple to stay on the program for life. The simple food column method presented in chapter eight is a great starting point.

Care-Free Stomach

Your body cannot tell the difference between the protein in a chicken breast or the protein contained in fish or even plant derived soy powder. Likewise, the fat contained in almonds or cashews is very similar to the fat found in avocados or olive oil. One gram of carbohydrate from a chocolate bar is essentially the same as one gram of carbohydrate from a slice of bread. Although you can taste the difference, your stomach has no emotional or political preference.

However, vitamins and minerals, or what are called micronutrients, will vary between foods. The program in this book serves to optimize your dietary intake of these important substances. Just remember though, it is the balance of fat, protein and carbohydrate that most significantly contributes to good health.

Most of what you eat contains some combination of the three macronutrients, however various foods are richer in one or more component. For example, milk is a protein rich food, and peanut butter is a fat rich food. Yet both of these also contain some amount of all three macronutrients: protein, fat and carbohydrate.

Food labels give a partial description of product ingredients. For example, the label of a typical box of shredded wheat shows that one serving (three pieces) contains 7 grams of protein, 1 gram of fat and over 50 grams of carbohydrate. A common corn cereal that contains a little less carbohydrate (24 grams) has a nutrition label as seen below.

Note that underneath the heading words "Nutrition Facts," you will see the words *"serving size,"* which in this case equals one cup. Therefore, you know that one cup of this product contains 24 grams of carbohydrate, two grams of protein and zero grams of fat. The other items listed are not overly relevant. Sometimes the challenge lies in finding the important information that is buried among other complicated looking distractions.

Nutrition Facts		
Serving Size	1 Cup (28g/1.0 oz.)	
Servings per Package	About 12	
	Cereal with ½ Cup Vitamins A & D	
Amount Per Serving	Cereal	Skim Milk
Calories	100	140
Calories from Fat	0	0
	**% Daily Value **	
Total Fat 0g*	0 %	0 %
Saturated Fat 0g	0 %	0 %
Cholesterol 0mg	0 %	0 %
Sodium 200mg	8 %	11 %
Potassium 25mg	1 %	7 %
Total Carbohydrate 24g	8 %	10 %
Dietary Fiber 1g	4 %	4 %
Sugars 2g		
Other Carbohydrate 21g		
Protein 2g		

Any good food count book, such as Corinne T. Netzer's *The Complete Book of Food Counts*, will also tell you how many grams of each macronutrient is contained in hundreds of different foods. As mentioned, most foods contain some combination of the three macronutrients.

The following table provides basic information about the *dominant* content of common foods:

Protein:

Meat, poultry, seafood, fish, cheese, eggs, tofu.

Soybean imitation meats (hotdogs, burgers, deli slices).

Protein powders (milk, whey, egg, soybean).

Milk and yogurt (also about 1/2 carbohydrate).

Fats:

Oils (olive, canola, peanut, etc.).

Butter, margarine, cheese spreads.

Regular mayonnaise or salad dressing.

Cream, sour cream, most nuts and seeds.

Avocados, olives, bacon strips, fried foods.

Carbohydrates:

Fruits, vegetables and legumes.

Almost all types of juice, including vegetable juice. All sugar sweetened soft drinks.

Breads, muffins, cereals, pasta, rice, other grains, cookies, cakes, candies, chips, etc.

Hundreds of prepared and packaged foods.

Milk and yogurt (also about 1/2 protein).

You can see from the previous table that fruits and vegetables are listed in the carbohydrate section along with breads, muffins and cereals etc. Please make note that vegetables, and to a lesser extent fruit, contain far fewer grams of carbohydrate than the equivalent amount of pasta, bread or rice. For example, one cup of cooked pasta contains about 40 grams of carbohydrate, compared to the 4 grams contained in one cup of broccoli.

While learning about proteins, fats and carbohydrates are important, calorie counting is less significant. How can this be true? Doesn't health have a lot to do with weight and isn't weight about counting calories? Don't fat people simply eat more calories and exercise less than thin people? If this were true then why are there so many inactive thin people who can eat whatever they wish and not gain weight? The next chapter will explain the powerful role hormones play in appetite, weight control, illness and energy levels.

3.

Basic Hormone Facts

Where all think alike, no one thinks very much.

Walter Lippman

The Balancing Act

Human hormone systems are complex, yet it is easy to understand the concept of balance. The body is continuously trying to produce the correct mix of chemical hormones that will enable your entire system to function properly. This involves creating not too much and not too little of any one substance. Your body chemistry works best within certain ranges. Staying within these measurable ranges contributes to both physical and mental health.

Natural chemicals made within your cells and organs form intricate feedback loops that control such things as fat storage, blood sugar, acid levels, enzymes and much more. Fortunately, once you understand the relationship between food and hormones, you will be better able to control and balance your own body chemistry.

What Are Hormones?

The word "hormone" is derived from the Greek verb *hormao* meaning to excite or arouse. In short, hormones are substances that arouse or stimulate hundreds of reactions within your body. Such things as sleep, emotional stress, exercise, alcohol, medications, caffeine and even smoking will affect these chemical messengers.

Hormones are the orchestra conductors of human life. They influence pain, mood, weight, fertility, sleep, digestion, immunity, energy levels, and more. Hormones can even alter the structure of your hair, skin, muscles and bones. These 24-hour a day messengers are produced by glands such as the pancreas, thyroid, adrenal and others. Like an army of soldiers, each carrying specific instructions, they control virtually every aspect of human physiology.

Food plays a powerful role in controlling hormone balance. Specifically, it is the amount of carbohydrates, proteins and fats consumed that have well documented hormonal results. Scientists have repeatedly measured the swift and predictable effects that certain food components have on various hormones. For example, we know that 100 calories of cornflakes has a very different hormonal effect than 100 calories of olive oil.

Two of the most important hormones related to food are insulin and glucagon. Anyone specializing in the area of diabetes, heart disease, arthritis or even cancer will be aware of the power of these metabolic messengers. For example, scientists have known for decades that excess insulin is strongly linked to such things as strokes, heart attacks, amputations, retinopathy (eye damage), neuropathy (nerve damage), kidney disease and other ailments. Glucagon, however, is the biological opposite of insulin. So let's look more closely at both insulin and glucagon.

Insulin

Insulin is produced near your stomach by a fist-sized organ called the pancreas. The pancreas is like a production factory that is ready to release insulin whenever your body demands it. And what has the *most* influence over how much insulin your body demands? It is the amount of carbohydrate you consume. And you can forget the old fashion terms "simple" or "complex." A carbohydrate is a carbohydrate, when it comes to making insulin.

Carbohydrate foods contain various forms of sugar, including fructose found in fruit, galactose found mainly in dairy products and glucose from bread, pasta, cereals and starchy vegetables. Sugar has many different names and forms but once eaten all sugars eventually change into a type of fuel your body can most easily use. This energy source is called glucose.

Just as gasoline fuels your car, glucose fuels your body. For simplicity's sake, it can be helpful to think of glucose, carbohydrates, starch, and sugars as all meaning the same thing. In fact, all carbohydrates are merely different forms of simple sugars joined together by chemical bonds. Your stomach can't tell the difference. Even corn, potatoes, baked beans and bread are all quickly changed into glucose. They are similar, in many ways, to common white sugar.

So when you eat these and other carbohydrate foods, your pancreas releases insulin. Insulin then works like a key to unlock the muscle and fat cells and allow glucose to enter. Too much glucose entering the cells is stored as body fat. On the other hand, the complete absence of insulin causes extreme weight loss and eventual death.

Scientists call insulin an anabolic hormone, which means that it has the ability to promote the build-up of stored fat. But eating carbohydrates does not necessarily make us overweight or sick. What makes us overweight or sick is the common habit of eating too much food. This occurs when we do not understand what our body *requires* to feel satisfied. If you first give your body what it really *needs*, then it will be far less likely to crave more food. Feed your need and you will succeed.

As well, the more carbohydrates we eat, the more we want to eat and the more insulin is released.

Insulin: the storage hormone

Scientists know that about three-fourths of the population cannot tolerate eating excess carbohydrates. Physicians have labeled this pre-diabetic condition as glucose intolerance. This problem, along with Type II diabetes, is strongly linked to obesity. Such people are born with a genetic tendency to releasing excess insulin. Doctors describe this as the "thrifty gene" problem. People with this genetic makeup survive in times of famine because they easily store body fat.

Some of this fat also gets deposited in arteries and other blood vessels. This leads to the narrowing of the passageway for blood flow and can result in high blood pressure, strokes, heart attacks and other disorders. One of the biggest myths of nutrition is that dietary fat is the primary villain that clogs our arteries. This is simply not true, as revealed in an August 1997 article in the *New England Journal of Medicine*. It is excess glucose and insulin that dangerously narrows or completely blocks (causing strokes) our blood vessels.

At this point, you may start to wonder why I am continuing to write about diabetes. Without going into details, just know that diabetes and insulin levels have a great deal to do with blood circulation and well-being. You will soon see how this relates to overall mental and physical health, not merely diabetes.

We all need a certain amount of insulin to enable us to use food for energy. People with Type II diabetes initially make too much insulin while those with Type I cannot make any insulin at all. Type I diabetes represents an excellent model for demonstrating the power of hormones over body weight. A person with untreated (no insulin injections) Type I diabetes can eat enormous amounts of food and actually lose weight to the point of death.

Early 1921 photographs of young diabetics at The Hospital for Sick Children in Toronto show painfully thin, near death figures. This was a common occurrence prior to the 1922 Canadian discovery of injectable insulin. Toronto physicians, Banting and Best, isolated insulin from the pancreas of dogs. This eventually led to the use of life saving insulin injections. Without insulin treatment, children with Type I diabetes literally starved to death, even though they ate plenty of food.

How is weight loss and even starvation possible when large amounts of food are being eaten? Think of a car whose fuel tank is not connected to the engine. You keep adding more and more gasoline to the car, but it won't run because the fuel isn't getting to where it is needed. Similarly, humans must

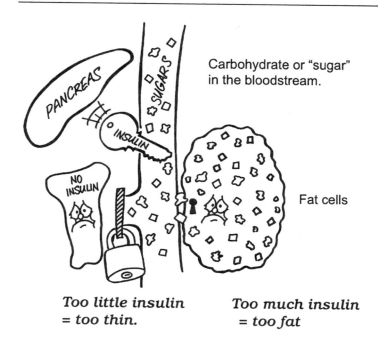

Carbohydrate or "sugar" in the bloodstream.

Fat cells

Too little insulin = too thin.   **Too much insulin = too fat**

eat food for fuel and insulin is like a connecting pipe from the fuel (food) to the engine. Without insulin, the fuel cannot get to where it is needed and there is no energy, no fat storage and no life. Insulin is like a *key* that unlocks the cells of your body to allow "storage" of your body weight.

What does this have to do with you? While you may not have Type I diabetes, your weight and health remain strongly influenced by how much insulin your body makes. Eat too many grams of carbohydrate and you will make too much insulin. If you continually make excess insulin, you will feel mentally foggy, tired and sick.

In fact, a 1994 study published in the *Journal of the American Dietetic Association* states that "hyperinsulinemia (too much insulin) is largely responsible for hunger, cravings and weight gain observed in many obese." They conclude that "an eating program focused on reduction of chronic hyperinsulinemia, along with exercise and behavior modification, can successfully and permanently bring down cravings, hunger and body weight."

As mentioned earlier, about three-fourths of the population cannot tolerate a high carbohydrate diet and often end up with Type II diabetes. These people typically make too much insulin, which is further prevented from working properly when excess fat surrounds the body cells. This complex condition is called insulin resistance.

The combination of hyperinsulinemia and insulin resistance is extremely dangerous. Such people often have high LDL (bad) cholesterol, high blood pressure, high blood fats (not caused by dietary fat) and other abnormal findings. These measurable tests are well known to be important risk factors for chronic pain, heart disease, strokes, obesity, cancer and other disorders. High insulin levels even influence autoimmune conditions such as arthritis and multiple sclerosis (see chapter seven).

The majority of people with high blood insulin levels are overweight. Yet there are exceptions. For example, some thin people have a combination of hyperinsulinemia, high blood pressure, high triglycerides and a family history of heart disease. These people are the genetic exceptions. They can eat a great deal and not gain weight, yet they still benefit from dietary intervention that controls insulin.

Stress can also cause an increase in insulin secretion. The award winning Banting lecture presented at the 1997 American Diabetes Conference confirmed that even moderate stress can increase the hormone epinephrine, which causes the liver to release significant amounts of glucose. And when glucose is dumped into the blood stream it stimulates insulin.

Stress can raise insulin levels.

Exercise, on the other hand, lowers insulin by making cells more sensitive to the uptake of this hormone. Exercise enhances the action of insulin during physical activity and for several hours afterwards. Any athlete with Type I diabetes can confirm this statement. Unfortunately, exercise motivation is typically low for those who follow a high carbohydrate diet. The resulting fatigue will turn off even the most disciplined person. So let's summarize:

Too much insulin:

1) Makes you gain weight

2) Makes it difficult to lose weight

3) Results mainly from eating too much carbohydrate (breads, pasta, potatoes etc.)

4) Makes you feel chronically tired and hungry

5) Increases fat deposits in blood vessels, thereby decreasing blood oxygen and nutrient delivery

6) Is related to a multitude of chronic illnesses

Now let's look at the second key hormone that is primarily controlled by food. This is called glucagon.

Glucagon

Glucagon removes stored body fat

Glucagon works in an opposite way to insulin, by acting to release stored body fat. Think of glucagon as being like money you put in a candy machine. Put a coin in and the candy is released. The candy is like excess body fat. When you add glucagon to your bloodstream, excess body fat is easily released.

Insulin and glucagon are continuously being balanced in an effort to control your body size. Short of amputation, it is impossible to lose weight without sufficient amounts of blood glucagon. Eating too many grams of carbohydrate will prevent glucagon production.

Exercise, however, increases the release of glucagon. Glucagon helps to stimulate a powerful fat burning substance known as human growth hormone. Regular moderate weight training, as opposed to aerobic exercise, is the best way to stimulate growth hormone. Just minutes a day with light weights will do the trick.

Ironically, this great health and weight loss hormone, glucagon, is also stimulated indirectly by eating dietary fat! How is this possible? Doesn't eating fat make you fat? The answer is no. Eating fat causes the release of a hormone called cholecystokinin which stimulates glucagon production. More good news about food fat is revealed in chapter six.

Glucagon also acts to raise metabolic rate or what is known as resting body temperature. Your food intake affects how tolerant you are to sudden changes in temperature. In addition, normal aging involves some loss of ability to adjust your internal body thermostat, but proper food intake can diminish this problem.

Glucagon also plays a role in helping muscles to contract, especially your heart muscle. Physicians talk about glucagon "exerting a positive inotropic effect on the heart" which simply means that it helps the heart to beat more efficiently. A chronically low glucagon level combined with too much insulin is definitely a heart health hazard. In fact, high blood insulin is the *single greatest* independent risk factor for heart disease.

So how do we ensure that our body is making enough, but not too much, of this important hormone? Having little food available is one solution, but this is seldom the case for North Americans. And too little food also results in a shortage of vitamins and minerals. Part of the solution is to consume the right amount and combination of nutrient dense foods.

Protein also causes the release of glucagon. And eating a little of the protein portion of your meal *first* acts to stimulate the release of glucagon in preparation for balancing insulin. So it makes good sense to nibble on small protein appetizers such as cheese, fish or meat hors-d'oeuvres and avoid those carbohydrate loaded bread rolls. The world's most sophisticated cuisines typically includes miniature protein appetizers, not all-you-can-eat bread or pasta. So whenever you eat, chew slowly and *begin* with a bite of some protein rich food.

As you may have guessed, glucagon is also released during periods of starvation. This allows the body to use stored energy from fat and liver cells. This starvation backup mechanism is designed to meet your brain's demand for glucose. Chronically skipping meals, however, only acts to slow metabolic rate and increase the risk of eventual over eating.

Periodic starvation, or going off and on ultra low calorie diets is a surefire way to eventually *gain weight* and lose health. Moreover, most low calorie diets are also low in essential nutrients, including protein, fat, vitamins, minerals and trace minerals. Nutrient starvation makes your body crave more food. Few people, when given the choice, are able to stick with any excessively low fat, low calorie and nutrient poor diet.

If food is chronically unavailable, or for some reason refused, then continued starvation causes the breakdown of muscle fibers. This muscle loss provides the brain with critically needed fuel. Such is the case with the tragic illness, anorexia nervosa.

Similarly, people with untreated Type I diabetes are unable to make insulin and become extremely thin. They also develop high blood levels of a substance known as ketones. This can result in a deadly condition called ketoacidosis, but this is typically found only in those with untreated Type I diabetes.

The average person has nothing to fear from small amounts of blood ketones. Ketones are not, as commonly believed, "poison to your body." In fact, the body is quite happy to use some ketones as a source of fuel.

The world renowned Johns Hopkins Medical Center has even used ketogenic diets to treat a variety of conditions, including epilepsy. Patients using this approach often eliminate the need for seizure medication, such as Dilantin (call 1-800-for-keto).

On the other hand, some researchers believe that *excess* ketones cause irreversible changes to fat cells, making them even more prone to attracting and storing fat. Balance is the key. So let's summarize what we know about glucagon.

Glucagon:

1) Helps control body temperature

2) Helps the heart to beat more efficiently

3) Helps other muscles to contract

4) Acts to release and remove excess body fat

5) Stimulates the secretion of human growth hormone

6) Is released in response to cholecystokinin (a hormone secreted after eating dietary fat)

7) Increases in the blood stream after eating protein

8) Increases during and after exercise

Brain and Blood Sugar

The human brain depends on a minute to minute supply of a type of sugar, mentioned earlier, called glucose. Blood glucose levels affect our mental and physical energy, susceptibility to headaches, hunger and much more. High blood glucose levels will even slow down wound healing. To simplify matters we will use the term blood glucose and blood sugar to mean the same thing.

When blood sugar levels are too high we tend to experience fatigue, thirst, dry mouth, inability to concentrate and frequent urination. On the other hand, if blood sugar is too low we experience symptoms such as headaches, hunger, trembling, sweating, blurred vision or sudden fatigue. Feelings of well-being occur when blood sugar is not too high and not too low.

Symptoms of low blood sugar:

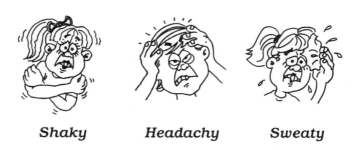

Shaky **Headachy** **Sweaty**

Blood sugar levels outside the normal range cause our brain to signal that *something is wrong and urges us to fix the problem.* Unfortunately, too many of us turn to self-medication with alcohol, tobacco, caffeine or other drugs. Or we overeat. We are naturally trying to feel better fast.

Yet these solutions offer only a temporary fix that meet our short-term comfort needs. They do nothing to promote ongoing health. Drugs, caffeine, alcohol, smoking, overeating and inactivity all contribute to poor health. So why do so many keep up the punishment? Doing the right thing does not need to be difficult once we gain some understanding.

The irony is that living a healthy lifestyle can be easy and becomes easier once we experience success. Setting and achieving small short-term goals helps us to work smarter, not harder. You needn't suffer from lack of concentration, hunger, deprivation or anxiety. Slowly and consistently developing a few healthy habits will improve your life.

Moreover, the *minimum* foundation for mental and physical health involves meeting your brain's energy requirements. Any endocrinologist will tell you that the human brain functions best within a narrow and measurable range of blood sugar (specifically 70–100 mg per 100 ml or 3.8–7.0 mmol/l of blood). This can be measured by using a blood glucose meter.

Supplying your brain with a consistently adequate amount of blood glucose (sugar) is an important part of emotional stability. Yet this does not mean we must eat sugar or plenty of carbohydrate loaded foods. The body is able to convert many different foods into blood sugar, including protein and fat.

Psychiatrist and author Dr. Michael Norden often recommends a carbohydrate restricted dietary approach for his patients. His book *Beyond Prozac* describes this food prescription as being a successful treatment for certain types of depression.

Mental illness is complex and there is no single cure, but balancing our food intake contributes to emotional stability.

As well, it is ironic that your brain may be starving for sugar, even while you are eating plenty of sugary junk food. This occurs because too much carbohydrate releases excess insulin, which then acts to drive down blood sugar levels. Your brain then says, "Where's my fuel?" Worse still is the fact that most of that blood sugar is being stored away as excess body fat. Yet we still feel hungry!

Scientists have proven that chronically high blood sugar levels cause significant health problems. A recent long term, multi-center study called the Diabetes Complication and Control Trial (DCCT) showed that chronically elevated blood glucose causes serious damage to our bodies. The results of this seven-year study were not surprising. Decades earlier, the father of diabetes care, Dr. Elliot P. Joslin, expressed similiar beliefs.

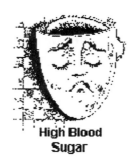

High Blood Sugar

Living with high blood sugar, (typically preceded by high insulin levels) will eventually damage the heart, blood vessels, eyes, nerves, kidneys, and other body organs. Elevated blood glucose is currently the leading cause of blindness in North America. However many people with vague symptoms such as fatigue or blurred vision may simply believe this to be a normal part of aging.

In addition, low blood sugar, known as hypoglycemia, can also cause problems. While true hypoglycemia usually occurs in people taking prescription drugs, symptoms of this condition can exist without medication. Those who are carbohydrate sensitive may not show significant numerical evidence of hypoglycemia, yet they can still experience distressing symptoms. The dietary suggestions in this book will help people with hypoglycemia.

So how do we supply our brain with an adequate and steady supply of blood sugar? How can we maintain mental alertness, boost our immunity and feel energetic? The answer is to regularly eat the correct amount of high quality protein mixed with low glycemic carbohydrates (explained later) and the right kind of fat. You will then be well on your way to achieving optimal blood sugar levels. Details of these steps can be found in chapter eight.

Controlling both insulin and blood glucose are critical components of good health. Consider how feeling clear headed and alert can literally affect almost every aspect of your life. Your ability to concentrate, to work, to play, to exercise, to avoid illness, to enjoy good relationships and to create a successful life are all influenced by blood glucose and insulin levels.

Master Hormones

We've just looked at how glucagon and insulin act to balance blood sugar, but what acts to control glucagon and insulin? The answer is a group of master hormones known as the eicosanoids (eye-cos-a-noyds). Few health professionals are aware of these fascinating substances, yet the medical literature is brimming with relevant information. For example, a current one-year Medline search revealed over 200 scientific papers detailing how eicosanoids affect human health.

Biochemist Dr. Barry Sears first popularized their understanding in his thought provoking book, *Enter the Zone.* He highlighted their importance by emphasizing that the 1982 Nobel Prize in Medicine was won for eicosanoid research. The bottom line is that understanding how to control eicosanoids is an important key to quality of life and longevity. The Nobel Prize has never been awarded for trivial discoveries.

Dr. Sears work stimulated my interest in eicosanoids. I began to look more closely at these little known hormones and the more I read, the more convinced I became about the role of diet in controlling their action.

Furthermore, through a chance encounter, I met Dr. Bob Bruce, Professor of Nutrition at the University of Toronto. Dr. Bruce, at age 70, has spent most of his career studying food and its relationship to health. A phone conversation confirmed that he believed Dr. Sear's ideas were credible. In fact, Dr. Bruce and his wife Margaret, a Registered Dietitian, both altered their food intake in a way that controls eicosanoid balance. They are delighted with the results.

In addition, the President of the Ontario Heart and Stroke Foundation, Mr. Rick Gallop, followed Dr. Sear's ideas and shed 17 pounds. He was so excited about his new carbohydrate restricted lifestyle that he told many of his colleagues about the discovery. Evidence was building.

In addition, I telephoned the office of Dr. Walter C. Willett, head of nutrition at the prestigious Harvard School of Public Health. I asked Cathy, his assistant, if Dr. Willett supported the Zone food concepts. She told me that the professor was in Europe but that she would call back. One week later I received a message confirming that Dr. Willett believed Dr. Sears book presented "sound guidelines for healthy eating."

When a Harvard nutrition professor disagrees with government supported dietary guidelines, one tends to question what is going on. My conviction grew stronger.

All this is not to imply that everyone should eat a strict "Zone diet." Despite what critics

Evidence from Harvard and the University of Toronto

say, Dr. Sears understands the psychological and genetic aspects of nutrition and he supports flexibility. His valuable contribution was to emphasize that good health requires consuming a certain range of the right kind of protein, fat and nutrient dense foods. He also makes people realize how easy it is to overconsume sugar in the form of bread, bagels and pasta. As well, though controversial to some, his explanation of eicosanoids makes perfect sense to those who understand diabetes and other chronic illnesses.

So just what are these eicosanoids? They are extremely powerful hormones that exist in your blood stream for fleetingly short periods of time. They cannot easily be measured and their elusive nature makes them difficult to study. Yet they are produced by almost every cell in your body and are the essential communication links between cells.

Some of the most common eicosanoids include:

1) prostaglandins

2) leukotrienes

3) thromboxanes and

4) arachidonic acid

Eicosanoids can be described as either favorable or unfavorable and like many health factors, it is a *balance* of these hormones that is important. For example, some eicosanoids prevent excessive bleeding by causing blood to clot. But too much clotting hampers circulation and may lead to a stroke or heart attack. If you are making too many unfavorable eicosanoids you will also increase the risk for uncontrolled cellular proliferation (cancer), while too few hamper normal cellular growth and repair.

Here is a summary of the two master hormones, as described by Dr. Sears:

Favorable Eicosanoids:	**Unfavorable Eicosanoids:**
• thin blood	• thicken blood
• dilate blood vessels	• constrict vessels
• decrease blood pressure	• increase pressure
• decrease pain sensation	• increase pain
• decrease inflammation	• inflame tissues
• boost immunity	• depress immunity

Hundreds of scientific studies have shown that people suffering from a variety of chronic illnesses are producing high levels of unfavorable eicosanoids. We also know that *the most critical factor in creating unfavorable eicosanoids is the overproduction of insulin.*

Do you still have doubts about the power of food to heal or prevent illness? If so, then consider that the only consistently proven method of increasing the life span in a variety of animals is through dietary control. This control involves providing adequate levels of protein, fat, vitamins and minerals, while *restricting carbohydrates.* More about this in chapter eight, but first we need to have a close look at carbohydrates, protein and fat.

4.

Carbo Common Sense

> People have the mistaken belief that as long as they're eating carbohydrates, they won't add inches to their waistline.
>
> Dr. W. Willett,
> Harvard School of Public Health

Conventional Food Advice

Over the past 15 years, both government guidelines and persuasive food advertising have influenced North American dietary habits. Cultural conditioning has made us believe that good health results from avoiding fat and eating lots of carbohydrate. The American food pyramid teaching tool encourages people to fill up on breads, grains and starches. The Canadian version, called the Rainbow Food Guide, also encourages consumption of

41

5-12 portions of grain products daily. Both of these are widely used by professional dietitians.

Surely these conventional recommendations can't be wrong, or can they? If conventional advice is correct, then why are North Americans heavier, sicker and more depressed than ever? Humans are simply not designed to eat plenty of carbohydrate, especially wheat based products.

Unfortunately, since carbohydrates are cheap, readily available, and tasty, they are easy to over consume. Long lasting carbohydrates are also attractive to the food industry. What could be better for business than paying a few cents for the raw materials, such as sugar, and adding some flashy packaging and charging a high price? Most dry cereal boxes cost more to produce than the contents of the package.

Meanwhile, longevity studies have shown that the key to better health lies in getting sufficient nutrients while eating less total food. And while scientists know that there are essential amino acids (proteins) and essential fats, no one has ever written about an essential carbohydrate. "Essential" means that your body needs it for survival. If you succeeded in getting rid of all the fat or all the protein in your diet, you would be dead in a few months. Humans can survive quite well on very little carbohydrate. The traditional Inuit (Eskimo) diet is a good example and autopsies done on elderly Inuits show them to have the arteries of a typical teenager.

As mentioned earlier, high blood glucose or high insulin levels cause many chronic health problems.

In addition, a 1994 position statement from the American Dietetic Association states: "*the most critical factor affecting blood glucose is the total number of grams of carbohydrate consumed.*" Control the amount of carbohydrate you eat and you will help to control blood sugar and insulin.

This, in turn, strengthens immunity and decreases our risk for getting things like colds and flu. Even our chances of getting cancer and other serious disorders are affected by the strength of our immunity. Fortunately, many severe cancer treatments such as radiation and chemotherapy are gradually being replaced by methods aimed at rallying the immune system. These treatment options have been referred to as biological defense modifiers. They are some of the fastest growing fields of medical research.

High blood glucose is also known to increase the risk of infections and contribute to slow wound healing. Diabetic amputee and ulcer patients often spend months in hospital. This slow wound healing stems from the inability of white blood cells to effectively act in the presence of high blood sugar.

Vitamin and Mineral Source

Virtually every nutritionist supports the idea of encouraging people to eat fibrous vegetables. This is partly because it is very hard to overconsume carbohydrates in the form of vegetables.

Anyone can breeze through a cup of pasta, but eating 8 cups of broccoli is another story. Both, however, contain about the same amount of glucose producing carbohydrate.

Consuming vegetables and fruit also maximizes our micronutrient intake of vitamins, minerals, and other health promoting plant chemicals. These micronutrients are almost non-existent in such things as pasta, white bread or polished rice.

Therefore, eating a diet rich in fruits and vegetables diminishes your need for supplementation. It is, however, inexpensive insurance to take 400-1200 IU per day of vitamin E. As Harvard's Dr. Walter Willett says, "It is almost impossible to get adequate amounts of vitamin E on a low fat meal plan."

A daily multivitamin and mineral supplement can also be useful. Yet high doses of any vitamin or mineral will do more harm than good. Our bodies only need small amounts of these substances. That's why they're called "micro" nutrients. So popping too many pills and potions is both a waste of money and can even result in depressing your immunity.

Carbs and Portion Size

Carbohydrates include many foods such as fruits, most vegetables, sugars, syrups, jams, breads, cereals, pasta, rice and much more. Ideally, at least three-fourths of your total carbohydrates should come from fruits and vegetables. You may wish to consume the other quarter in the form of dense (concentrated) carbohydrates such as pasta, cereals, rice or similar products. Portion size for these less favorable foods must be smaller than what you might be use to. You may also find it better to completely avoid these concentrated carbs.

How do you know if you are eating about three-fourths of your carbohydrates in the form of fruits and vegetables? One way is to become familiar with how many grams of carbohydrate are in the foods that you commonly like to eat. You can do this quite easily by filling in the personalized food chart in the appendix. A simpler but slightly less accurate way is to choose, as often as possible, from the starred selections in the food column list found in chapter eight. You can also use the easy palm size method described in the same chapter.

Filling in your personal food chart and *doing the numbers* for the foods you regularly like to eat will lead to some surprising conclusions. Learn to enjoy quality. Free yourself to savor the subtle tastes of food rather than overwhelming your palate with sugar and starch. With the right planning, you can create hearty meals that look appetizing and taste great.

Wheat and Restaurant Conditioning

Ph.D. pharmacologist and Barbados physician, Dr. Robert Gaskin, has evidence to suggest that wheat based food products are at the root of many chronic illnesses. He also believes that his own racial makeup as a black person exaggerates the problem. "Most blacks," he states, "are genetically intolerant of wheat based food products." Nutrition Professor David Jenkins has also found that white flour contributes to persistently high blood sugar.

Hold the Flour!

Unfortunately, restaurant size portions have conditioned us to eat large amounts of, what is essentially, sugar. Most restaurants serve plenty of dense carbohydrates such as bread, rice, pasta and potatoes because they are a relatively inexpensive way to fill up your plate. On the other hand, serving plenty of lobster or salmon would require charging a higher price that may not appeal to the average consumer.

Becoming aware of our cultural conditioning is a big step toward better health. Compare, for example, the portion size of European food versus American food. American advertisers promote more of an "all you can eat" philosophy, especially when it comes to such things as cakes, pretzels, cheesies and chips. Food companies succeed when they advertise and sell plenty of "keep 'em hungry" snacks.

"Here is your big plate of cheap carbs (bread, potatoes, pasta), so I can make a good profit"

So how much carbohydrate should we be eating? Restaurants won't give you the answer, nor will food advertisers. The food column list in chapter eight provides you with reasonable portion sizes and you can also use the palm of your hand as a guide. For example, if you must eat pasta, an appropriate meal serving is a rather flat, palm of your hand sized amount. The typical restaurant size plate of pasta is a health hazard.

In fact, a 1992 study published in the *International Journal of Cancer* found that Italians with the highest intakes of pasta also had the highest incidence of colon and rectal cancer. Yet no newspapers or television headlined this association. Indeed, the politics of pasta and grain bashing is counter-productive to the economic importance of these foods. Money talks and *is heard.* Business will pay to influence your belief system.

Carbs and Sugar Speed

We are using the term *sugar speed* to describe what scientists call the glycemic index. This index is nothing more than a measure of how fast carbohydrates turn into blood sugar. If a food has a high sugar speed then it turns into blood glucose (a type of sugar) faster than food that has a lower sugar speed. The faster our food turns into glucose, the faster we release insulin. So one way to control insulin is to eat foods with low sugar speeds.

How do we know how fast various foods turn into blood sugar? Dr. David Jenkins and his University of Toronto collegues measured this in the early 1980's. His team documented how quickly blood sugar rose in response to hundreds of different foods. Entire books have been written on this topic, so our purpose here is to present a few key points.

You do not need to know the exact sugar speed of every food. Simply become familiar with the foods you typically use. For example, liquids such as fruit juice turn into blood sugar more quickly than solid food, such as a piece of fruit. Low sugar speed foods are preferred and have been marked with a star in chapter eight.

The appendix also contains information on specific foods and their general sugar speeds. For example, fat free pasta turns into blood sugar faster than a plum or a pear. Similarly, one tablespoon of raisins and one-half an apple both contain 9 grams of carbohydrate, yet the raisins will raise your blood sugar more quickly than the apple. Apples have a low sugar speed because they contains a soluble form of fiber known as pectin.

Raw foods also tend to turn into sugar more slowly than overcooked foods. In addition, eating fresh and raw foods, when possible, maximizes vitamin and mineral content. Brief cooking times, however, can improves digestibility. Tolerance to raw foods will vary.

Harvard Professor of nutrition, Dr. Walter Willett, has emphasized that such things as white bread, pasta and potatoes should be put in the "eat less" top portion of the American food pyramid. These and other quickly absorbed carbohydrates behave in a manner similar to pure maple syrup. In short, they contain a form of sugar that enters the blood stream very quickly. Mash your potatoes or slather white bread with jam and you create an even higher sugar speed and higher insulin response.

Remember too that descriptions of "simple" or "complex" carbohydrates are misleading. The advertisers of a popular corn cereal shout the benefits of "complex carbohydrates," yet the sugar in this grain enters your blood stream faster than liquid honey. Likewise, white rice turns into blood glucose faster than most chocolate bars. Unfortunately, some people still believe in the misguided notion of eating more "complex" instead of "simple" carbohydrates.

Weight and Health Surprises

Although the focus of this book is on improving health and energy, we cannot ignore the fact that obesity is, no pun intended, a growing problem. There are now more overweight Americans than there are normal sized Americans. Childhood obesity has increased by more than 50% in the past 10 years.

Obesity related diabetes, which is also called Type II diabetes, has been estimated to cost the United States well over 50 billion dollars per year. Not all fat people, however, have diabetes or high blood pressure or chronic disease. For example, the enormous Japanese Sumo wrestlers eat a great deal but rarely suffer from diabetes or other chronic illness. They also eat no wheat or wheat products. They are fat from eating too much total food, but their wheat free diet has a protective influence.

The human tendency to store fat and secrete insulin is also influenced by our genetic makeup. Research done in Quebec, Canada by Dr. Claude Bouchard suggests that genetics plays a significant role in determining obesity. He studied identical twins separated at birth and raised in different environments. The weights of identical adult twins remained remarkably similar. Such twins are born with the same genetic insulin response.

What Dr. Bouchard fails to mention is that each research twin was also raised in an environment where cheap, wheat based carbohydrates were plentiful and where media advertising encouraged inactivity and over consumption. None of Dr. Bouchard's

Twin Studies

subjects moved to Japan to eat a soy and fish based diet, live without television and do active manual labor. Genetics does play a role in obesity, but consciously taking charge of environmental influences will alter family tendencies.

Being born with a high insulin response does not mean we are doomed to be persistently overweight. Insulin can be lowered to improve health. And it is measurable health, not thinness, that is a worthwhile goal.

Any cardiologist or weight specialist can tell you about the carbohydrate, insulin, exercise dilemma. Most people benefit from exercise, but it is especially important for overweight heart patients. Conventional dietitians tell heart patients that dietary fat is bad and eating carbohydrates is good. This results in more fatigue and hunger. Fatigue puts the brakes on motivation.

Determined patients who do become more active usually struggle all the way. Forcing oneself to exercise while on a low fat, high carb diet is rarely enjoyable. This experience further reinforces the distaste for moving. People end up feeling guilty for not being disciplined enough to keep exercising. Hormonally correct food advice, not discipline, is the key.

5.

Protein Hunger Link

> We are protein.
>> Jean Anderson, M.S. and
>> Barbara Deskins, PhD., R.D.,
>> authors of The Nutrition Bible.

The Overlooked Nutrient

Protein is the foundation for all life. If you subtract water, bones and fat from the human body, you are left mainly with protein. Your muscle, skin, nails, eyes, blood, enzymes, immune, reproductive and endocrine systems all depend on protein for proper functioning. Dietary protein is essential for both growth and development.

Few people, however, know how much they are eating. We usually rely on "feeling" that we eat enough. How many grams of protein did you eat for breakfast? Regrettably, most health conscious North Americans have been conditioned to fear anything that contains fat, and that includes meat. Even protein rich eggs tend to be out of fashion.

In addition, conventional dietary advice tells us to consume about 15% of our calories from protein. No wonder health conscious people tend to think they are "probably getting enough." This makes it sound like we only need a small bit. But eat too little and you will become sick. *Our immunity or defense against illnesses relies on protein.* How much protein each of us needs will depend on body size, amount of lean muscle tissue and activity level.

You do not, however, need to count every gram of protein. Although the greater your precision, the better your results, you can still reap benefits by using the easy column method or the super simple palm size approach (see chapter eight). All you do is choose the foods you like to eat. Our food columns have done the calculating for you.

Meeting your protein requirements is easy. Just remember that for each of us there is a specific ideal range, not too much and not too little. And while it is true that many people eat too much protein, because they simply eat too much food, others suffer from a chronic deficiency.

The three North American groups most at risk for protein deficiency are those living in poverty, female athletes and people on low fat diets. The low-income group often fills up on inexpensive items such as bread, pasta, potatoes and other starchy foods. For example, the "tea and toast syndrome" is a well-known hazard for the impoverished elderly.

Typical dieters and female athletes may also avoid meat and dairy products because they contain fat. Their faulty logic says that since fat is high in calories, avoiding fat is the best way to become thin. Yet as Harvard Professor of Nutrition, Dr. Walter Willett says, "controlled trials have not supported the idea that high fat diets promote weight gain." In fact, his 1998 article in the *American Journal of Clinical Nutrition*, gives overwhelming support for this statement.

Animal or Vegetable Protein?

High quality protein is essential for good health. Although vegetarians can live long and healthy lives, evidence suggests that humans were designed to eat both meat and plants. We have canine shaped teeth designed for tearing meat. Even biblical reference supports the belief that we are omnivores (meat and plant eaters). We function best by eating a mix of low fat protein, fibrous vegetables, plant-derived fats and small amounts of fruit.

At the molecular level, the source of protein makes little difference. Your mind may care about taste and appearance, but your stomach has no emotional preference. Protein from rabbit meat is used in the same way as plant based soybean products. Our stomach acid cannot tell what kind of protein it is digesting.

Our teeth, saliva and gut eventually break down all protein contained in foods into a variety of amino acids. Twenty vital amino acids make up the structural component of almost every human cell. Of the twenty amino acids, your body can make only 11, while the other nine must be supplied in the food we eat. Our bodies contain up to 20,000 different kinds of proteins that are continually being renewed.

Dietary proteins are either complete or incomplete, depending on their number of amino acids. Regular consumption of complete protein is your best defense against illness. You can survive on incomplete proteins from plants, but they will not promote optimal growth, immunity, strength or longevity. Meat, fish, eggs and dairy products, however, are convenient forms of high quality protein.

There are also a wide range of soy-based imitation meat products such as soybean hamburger, deli slices, hotdogs, pepperoni and others. These are available in the fruit and vegetable or frozen food section of most grocery stores. They contain high quality protein that is quick to prepare and tasty. Just look at the label and make sure they have little or no carbohydrate.

For the environmentally conscious, soybeans also use land more efficiently than grazing animals. In fact, our small planet would be better off if humans ate more soy protein and a bit less meat. However, a strict vegetarian lifestyle is not biochemically superior.

There is also a problem with traditional vegetarian protein sources such as beans, peas, lentils and legumes. These typically contain large amounts of carbohydrate. They are also encased in fiber shells that act to limit the amount of protein your body can absorb. Protein from egg whites is absorbed far more easily than protein from beans. This becomes especially important as we grow older and lose some ability to absorb nutrients. So high fiber protein sources do not promote health.

Unfortunately, vegetarianism is often ballyhooed in the popular press as being the ideal, super-healthy way of living. Yet there is no scientific evidence to support the idea that vegetarians live longer or more energetic lives than moderate meat eaters. Vegetarians do die of cancer, heart disease and other illnesses and they live no longer, on average, than meat eaters.

Well-known vegetarian advocate, Linda McCartney, died from cancer at age 56. On the other hand, one of the world's oldest men, Bir Narayan Choudhury from Kathmandu, swore by a strict diet of pork, milk, yogurt and rice. Of course these are only two examples, yet long-term studies also show that vegetarianism is no guarantee of quality or quantity of life.

Furthermore, have you ever met an elite athlete, body builder or weight lifter who is a strict vegetarian? You may not consider yourself to be a weight lifter, but even repeated grocery or child carrying is made easier by eating adequate amounts of protein. Similarly, a September 1991 study published in the *Canadian Journal of Public Health* concluded that "lean meat in reasonable serving sizes poses no threat to health and is an extremely important source of nutrients."

Regrettably, defense of a meatless diet is often based on emotionalism. One popular vegetarian book begins by saying "put a rabbit and an apple in a crib with a baby and I'll give you a million dollars if the kid eats the rabbit." Are we suppose to believe that this means humans should be vegetarians? Such logic defies reason. Would the baby eat the apple? Would an asthmatic infant choose to take a life saving medication?

Strict vegetarian diets can also cause excessive flatulence (gas) and bowel movements. Yet vegetarians justifiably argue that animal protein sources may contain undesirable hormones. Animals bred for human consumption may also be injected with antibiotics in an attempt to prevent disease, just as plant produce is sprayed with pesticides. For these and other reasons, it is best (but not essential) to purchase range fed meats and organic vegetables.

.... is better.

All this being said, it is still possible to eat well without consuming any animal products. Doing so, however, will require a little extra planning, especially if you value variety. Those devoted to avoiding all animal products tend to pay a price in access and convenience. There is also good evidence for the benefits of eating fish. The bottom line, however, is to consume the right mix of macronutrients.

Cure Chronic Hunger

Protein can also *prevent us from overeating, since it is an appetite suppressant.* Studies have shown that animals have a remarkable ability to control their protein intake. If permitted, most animals will continue to eat until they have consumed a specific amount of this food component. If they are presented with protein rich foods, they simply eat less total food and fewer calories. If presented with protein poor foods, they will eat a greater volume of food until, once again, they have reached a specific level of protein intake.

Optimal health involves eating as little as possible, while still consuming sufficient protein, fat, vitamins and minerals. Dr. Harvey Anderson, former Dean of Medicine at the University of Toronto, has written extensively on the role of protein in the regulation of food consumption. Protein lessens food cravings. On the other hand, excess carbohydrate intake, especially from wheat and wheat products, leads to continued feelings of hunger.

In fact, chronic hunger is the most common initial complaint expressed by my overweight patients. Such people cannot be dismissed as just being lazy or weak willed. More often, they have simply made the wrong food choices based on faulty information. Most also need time to learn about reasonable food portions and what lack of hunger feels like. Psychological interventions found in chapter nine will also help.

As mentioned previously, eating the protein portion of your meal or snack *first* can give you a head start toward greater energy levels. Protein makes your pancreas release glucagon and the fatigue inducing insulin response is lessened. Furthermore, starting with protein and a little fat sends an early satisfaction signal to your brain. The sooner you feel satisfied, the less total food you are likely to eat. And eating less food, *while consuming enough nutrients* is what this game is all about.

6.

Media Fat Phobia

> Essential fatty acids are necessary for good health because they are the precursors of eicosanoids.
>
> Dr. W. Ganong in
> *Review of Medical Physiology*

Need for Fat

Animals fed a fat free diet fail to grow, develop skin and kidney lesions, have weakened immunity and become infertile. Humans also require adequate amounts of dietary fat. If you could avoid all dietary fat, you would be dead within a few months.

Yet North Americans have created an entire industry devoted to the condemnation of fat. Grocery store shelves are bulging with food labels that

61

display the supposed benefits of low fat or no fat foods. Many consumers believe that fat free equals good health. If fat free foods are so healthy then why are North Americans sicker and more depressed than ever?

Current physiology textbooks provide sound evidence for the necessity of fat. One of the most respected publications, entitled *Review of Medical Physiology*, also provides details concerning the significance of fat as it relates to eicosanoids. As you know from chapter three, eicosanoids are important hormonal messengers. Dietary fat forms the foundation for all eicosanoids. Without fat, there are no eicosanoids and no life. Fat is your friend in health.

Furthermore, not one research study has proven that eating fat makes you fat or sick. Dietary fat has been falsely blamed for causing everything from heart disease and diabetes to weight gain and cancer. Unfortunately, many well-intentioned health professionals have been barking up the wrong tree. Our focus on condemning fat has caused a great deal of pain and suffering.

Cultural Conditioning

> Sometimes a majority simply means that all the fools are on the same side.
>
> Thomas Alva Edison

People often form food beliefs from quick and simple bits of media information. Few people look closely at the details. This approach makes it easy to misinterpret popular advice. People are told to "eat a low fat diet" or "try to cut down on fat." What exactly does this mean? How much do we need? Even the message to "eat a balanced diet," rarely helps. More information is needed.

Top this with the fact that conventional health education aids, such as the food pyramid or rainbow food guide, are grossly misleading, and you end up with one big problem. Harvard's Dr. Willett supports this view in his recent article published in the *American Journal of Clinical Nutrition* entitled "The dietary pyramid: does the foundation need repair?"

Further confusion is created when television and newspapers spread a variety of messages about healthy eating. Again, there are rarely any numbers put to this advice. And how often have you heard information about quantities to suit your unique size and activity level? If you hear that you need about 15% of calories from protein, does this mean you need the same amount of protein as the athlete next door? Not likely.

One of the worse scenarios occurs when people interpret "low fat" to mean, "avoid all fat." Although eating a no fat diet is almost impossible, any ultra low fat dietary approach is dangerous. Fatigue and depression are common symptoms. I have worked with dozens of well-educated women, including pharmacists, lawyers and teachers who say, "I try to avoid all fat." It is no wonder that such people complain of multiple health problems.

Groups that have previously led the anti-fat movement include The American Cancer Society, The American Heart Association and The National Heart, Lung and Blood Institute. These groups have steadily emphasized the need to cut down on saturated fats. Unfortunately, a good portion of the general public has equated their warnings to mean, "avoid all fat." Furthermore, recent research suggests that even saturated fat is not as harmful as once predicted. It only becomes harmful when we simultaneously follow a high carbohydrate diet.

The more we focus on the fear of fat, the worse off we become. However, buying low fat foods is not inherently bad, but it often increases our risk of eating more sugar. For example, no fat salad dressing typically has added sugar to replace the taste of fat. In addition, the no fat cookie syndrome made some people believe that fat free, sugar loaded cookies were actually good for you.

Fat, Weight and Eating Disorders

By now you know that eating more sugar simply increases your insulin response and contributes to weight gain. While low fat foods can fit into a balanced diet, they are not the solution for weight problems. If no fat foods were the answer, then North Americans would be winning the war on obesity. Instead, we are the fattest people on earth.

Dr. Willett addressed this problem in a recent keynote speech to over 3,000 health professionals at the International Congress of Nutrition. He provided compelling evidence to support the idea that our over emphasis on low fat, high carbo- hydrate eating is contributing to obesity. He encouraged a return to eating sensible portions of "real foods" such as eggs, nuts, fish and meat. He outlined the dangers of over consuming trendy low and no fat products.

We cannot deny, however, that many North Americans do eat too much fat and too much total food. If we habitually over eat hamburgers, hot dogs, French fries, pizza, chips, cookies, cakes and other high fat delights, then we will be consuming both too much fat and the wrong kind of fat.

In addition, the junk foods just listed also con- tain large amounts of carbohydrate. In fact, fat alone has little taste appeal. Not too many people will eat a tub of lard, but layer it between sugar loaded pastry and it becomes appealing. Fat acts as a flavor enhancer, primarily for carbohydrates.

We are not, however, out to encourage fat glut- tony and balance is the key. It is possible to eat the occasional treat, without gorging on large amounts. People can savor a bit of gourmet, high fat ice cream without feeling compelled to down the entire car- ton. Even those who have described their eating as "out of control" have learned to take charge and enjoy small portions. Feed your need *first* and you will control your craving for more food.

It is also important to make psychological peace with fat. Eating fat does not cause heart disease, cancer, diabetes or any other dreaded ailment. Yet all these conditions are strongly linked to being overweight. So is it possible to eat a lot of fat and still be slim and healthy?

The answer is definitely yes. As early as 1865 author William Banting detailed his meat and fat based diet as a way to lose weight. And in 1958 Dr. Richard Mackarness wrote about a return to health on a high fat diet. Anthropologist Vilhjalmur Stefansson also regained vitality after returning to a similar Stone Age diet. So too, did diabetologist Dr. Richard K. Bernstein. And for over 20 years, New York physician Dr. Robert Atkins has proven that dietary fat does not make you fat. The list could go on and on.

The correct balance of food is the key to better health and no one food is all good or all bad. Such black or white thinking shrouds mealtime with both anxiety and guilt. Unfortunately, the powerful anti-fat message continues to cause emotional anxiety for North Americans and there is currently no end in sight.

Some people have told me that they finally lost weight because they "gave up dieting." This has typically meant a return to eating reasonable portions of such things as eggs, meat and nuts, instead of big portions of fat free "diet" foods. Their past notion of dieting included lots of rice cakes, fat free pasta, skim milk and carrot sticks. But skim milk contains more carbohydrate than whole fat cream and has a higher glycemic index than cream. No wonder these bland and high sugar speed diets don't succeed.

Even low fat advocate Dr. Dean Ornish admits that regular meditation is an essential part of the discipline needed to stick with a low fat diet. While meditation can contribute to well-being, following a healthy diet should not be so difficult as to demand this support. Any ultra low fat diet is simply too difficult to stick with. Repeated failure then lowers self-esteem and a harmful cycle is set into motion.

Furthermore, scientists know that the main killer in obesity related heart disease has little to do with dietary fat. Numerous studies have proven that high blood sugar and high insulin levels are the primary cause of atherosclerosis (hardening of the arteries). Yet the vast majority of people hold the mistaken notion that it is dietary fat that clogs our arteries and leads to ill health.

Even the eating disorders of bulimia and anorexia can begin with ultra low fat dieting. Although complex psychological issues are part of the picture, biochemical imbalance from severe fat restriction also plays a role. More information on eating disorders and depression can be found in chapter seven. Those interested in the topic are encouraged to read

"The Secret Language of Eating Disorders," by Peggy Claude Pierre.

How Much Fat?

While most conventional doctors still support the less than 30% fat approach, Dr. Willett, thinks it's time to scrap it. He says, "The type of fat is important for heart disease, but the total amount of fat is not, as long as people watch their total food intake."

In addition, humans have a natural craving for dietary fat. As University of Michigan nutrition Professor, Adam Drewnoski says, "Humans have an innate tendency to consume energy-dense foods." Trying to stay on an ultra low fat diet goes against every normal human survival instinct.

What Kind of Fat?

Fishing for good fat ...

... olive oil, tahini, almonds, avocados, peanut butter...

Not all fats are created equal. Authors Lambert-Lagace and Laflame emphasize this point in their book *Good Fat, Bad Fat*. Different fats affect human health in a variety of ways. So what kind of fat is preferred?

The majority of added dietary fat should come from sources that are rich in mono-unsaturates. These include such things as olive oil, avocados, olives, almonds, macadamia nuts, peanuts, tahini and others. A recent article in the *New England Journal of Medicine* states, "It appears prudent to replace the majority of saturated and trans fats (partially hydrogenated fats) by oils high in mono-unsaturated fats such as canola or olive oil."

Unfortunately, canola oil is also 10% alpha-linoleic acid which has a slight negative affect on one of the enzymes used to produce good eicosanoids. While canola oil is definitely a better health bet than margarine, most nutritionists prefer olive oil. If you dislike the olive taste, you can use the lighter varieties.

The typical olive oil based Mediterranean diet is strongly associated with longevity and a low incidence of both heart disease and cancer. Mono-unsaturated fats also increase insulin sensitivity. Greater sensitivity helps remove and control excess blood insulin, which you now know is vital for good health.

On the other hand, trans fats or partially hydrogenated fats should be avoided. These are commonly found in margarines, pies, cakes, cookies, French fries and other packaged foods. Read the label and steer clear of them.

Saturated fats are concentrated mainly in animal sources such as fatty meats and butter.

Lard, coconut, palm and palm kernel oil are also high in saturated fats. It is also plentiful in most cheap deli meats such as bologna and hot dogs, as well as many bakery goods and snack foods. Such foods tend to be low in nutrients and high in calories.

Yet even saturated fats when eaten with sufficient amounts of fibrous vegetables are not as harmful as once predicted. A recent study published in the *Journal of the American Medical Association* found that eating more fat, even saturated fat, seemed to protect some men from strokes.

There is no need to be overly fearful of saturated fat, as long as you watch your carbohydrate intake. For example, as a remarkable 50-year survivor of Type I diabetes, Dr. Richard Bernstein says "I have the lipid (fat) profile of an Olympic athlete." He eats a very low carbohydrate, high fibrous vegetable, fat as desired, diet. His previous low fat, high carbohydrate way of eating resulted in dangerous triglyceride and cholesterol levels and classic blood vessel damage. His many patients (including physicians) have achieved similar results.

Linoleic Acid and GLA

So what other fats are important? If we think of health as the body making more good eicosanoids than bad then we want to use fats that will tip this biochemical balance in our favor. In short, there are fats we can either add or avoid that will promote good eicosanoids and better health.

A well-documented series of biochemical reactions begins with the essential fatty acid called linoleic acid. Since linoleic acid is essential for survival and cannot be made by our body, we must eat it. Luckily, this is easy since almost every food contains some linoleic acid, especially high fat foods. Unfortunately, in order to benefit from linoleic acid, our bodies must first change this fat into a more active substance known as gamma linoleic acid (GLA). Humans require sufficient amounts of activated essential fatty acids such as GLA to make good eicosanoids.

Most adults have the ability to produce GLA, but certain circumstances slow down production. For example, alcoholics have been found to have less than 50% of normal GLA blood levels. Women suffering from premenstrual syndrome have been found to have as little as 20% of the normal level.

In addition, GLA is difficult to find in the average diet. Human breast milk is a rich source, but it has yet to be bottled by your local grocer! Luckily, slow cooking oatmeal, ground whole oats, or steel cut oats also contain small amounts. Eat one or two tablespoons (dry) daily, of any of these, and you will be helping yourself to sufficient amounts of GLA. Just add to yogurt with some no carb sweetener such as stevia.

Remember too that the amount of linoleic acid consumed is not as important as whether it can be changed into GLA. Does the linoleic acid in your food have a ticket to be made into this active substance? Fortunately, we know that the ticket master is an enzyme called *delta 6 desaturase.* When this enzyme is available and functioning properly, our linoleic acid has a good chance of being converted to beneficial GLA. So what does this mean?

It turns out that one of the main factors controlling whether there is enough enzyme, and therefore enough GLA in your system, is dietary protein. Eat very little high quality protein and you will keep this enzyme waiting at the ticket window. If the enzyme cannot enter the chemical pathway, then GLA, and therefore good eicosanoid production, is depressed. Another factor that holds back the key enzyme is, you guessed it, a high carbohydrate diet.

In addition, aging, stress and inactivity are well known to affect health, so it is not surprising to find that these also depress the availability of our critical enzyme. Although we can't stop aging, we can become more active, and there are dozens of ways to manage stress, such as meditation, yoga, visualization or relaxation techniques.

As well, certain types of fats also inhibit our delta-6 enzyme and therefore limit GLA production. Some have been mentioned earlier. These include:

Fats to Avoid

1) Trans fatty acids (partially hydrogenated fats)
2) Fatty foods high in arachidonic acid (too much fatty red meat and deli type meats)

3) Alpha Linolenic Acid (a type of omega-3 fat high in walnuts, flaxseed and flaxseed oil)

Arachidonic Acid

Your body needs a small amount of arachidonic acid, but too much will create health problems. Back to the balancing act. Furthermore, as biochemist Dr. Barry Sears says, "inject any other fatty acid into animals and nothing happens, but inject arachidonic acid into rabbits and they are dead within minutes."

Arachidonic acid is the raw material from which bad eicosanoids are formed. These include such things like PGE2 that can promote pain and lower immunity; thrombaxane A2, that contributes to strokes and heart attacks; and leukotrienes that worsen skin disorders such as eczema, psoriasis and allergic reactions.

Furthermore, Professor of Medicine at Oregon University, Dr. Scott Goodnight writes, "The fatty acid precursor of most prostaglandins is arachidonic acid." Specific types of prostaglandins are well known to promote pain and inflammation. Too much arachidonic acid produces an imbalance of prostaglandins which causes various complaints such as headaches, menstrual cramps, joint pain and more.

Finally, egg yolks also contain arachidonic acid. Some people are sensitive to yolks, but recent research published in the *Journal of the American College of Nutrition* by Dr. R. H. Knopp concludes that the majority of people can safely eat whole eggs. Medical case reports exist of people who regularly eat 25 eggs per day with no ill effect.

The real issue may be that eating that many eggs leaves little room for excess carbs. If you have doubts, then just use egg whites. These contain a high quality and easily absorbed form of protein.

Alpha linoleic Acid

The following chart highlights the type of fat we want more of (mono-unsaturates) and the type of fats to minimize (alpha-linoleic-acid).

Mono-unsaturates and Alpha Linoleic Acid (ALA) in Common Oils:

(From Highest to Lowest in Mono-unsaturates)

Oil	% Mono-unsaturated	% ALA
Olive	82	0
Hazelnut	76	0
Almond	65	0
Canola	60	10
Peanut	49	0
Sesame (light)	46	0

Oil	% Mono-unsaturated	% ALA
Walnut	28	9
Corn	27	1
Soybean	24	7
Sunflower	19	0
Flaxseed	16	57
Safflower	13	0

Oils that are low in mono-unsaturates, but high in omega-6 fatty acids include such things as safflower, soybean, corn and sunflower oils. They all sound so healthy. Yet use of these oils, without sufficient amounts of omega-3 fish oils, will tip the balance toward bad eicosanoids. Even the most conservative government supported food publications echo the same advice.

Flaxseeds

The previous chart shows that flaxseed oil contains a high percentage of alpha-linoleic acid. Health food stores promote flaxseed as the ultimate cure for everything from arthritis to menopausal symptoms. Indeed, the seed and its oils can provide quick symptomatic relief for a variety of conditions.

Unfortunately, relief is achieved by knocking out virtually all eicosanoid production, both good and bad. It's a little like chopping your foot off to treat an ingrown toenail. Similarly, would you take powerful drugs, like corticosteroids, if they relieved your pain but created a whole new set of problems? Millions of people do this daily.

In fact, a recent article in the *Journal of the American Medical Association* listed adverse reactions from prescribed drugs as the fourth leading cause of death in the United States. When you learn to follow our simple food guidelines, you will quickly discover how to prevent pain and avoid the need for most drugs.

Pills treat symptoms, not causes.

And finally, the amount of evidence for the benefits of omega-3 from fish fat compared to flaxseed oil is like comparing an elephant to an inchworm. Time to look more closely at fish.

The Good Fatty Fish

As early as 1908 Nobelist August Krogh described the Greenland Inuits as "the most exquisitely carnivorous people on earth." They were also an incredibly heart healthy population. In 1970,

this knowledge led chemists Jorn Dyerberg and H.O. Bang to cross the sea to Greenland in search of dietary clues to the prevention of heart disease. They found most Inuits to have relatively low plasma cholesterol and triglyceride levels. In addition, their blood did not clot (bind together) easily because it contained high levels of omega-3 fats.

Later discoveries set off a wave of interest in the health benefits of omega-3 fish fats. The typical Inuit, Japanese and Norwegian diets were of particular interest. Although these populations were found to consume a high cholesterol diet, they still enjoyed low rates of heart disease.

A variety of American populations have also been analyzed. For example, Dr. Martha Daviglus, lead researcher of a study published in the *New England Journal of Medicine*, tracked the diet of Chicago Factory Workers since the 1950's. She found that people who ate fish twice a week had a 42 % lower rate of heart attack.

Omega-3 fish also contain another fat known as eicosapentaenoic acid (EPA). The amount of scientific evidence for the health benefits of EPA is overwhelming. A simple Medline computer search reveals virtually hundreds of scientific papers devoted to this topic. For example, EPA has been found to lower the amount of cholesterol made by the liver and decrease blood platelet aggregation (thins the blood). EPA has also been successfully used to relieve the symptoms of arthritis and psoriasis.

A study published in the May, 1999 issue of *Archives of General Psychiatry* also found that fish oil can help ease the symptoms of bipolar disorder (manic depression). Dr. Andrew Stoll, the main author of the study, conducted at the Brigham and

Women's Hospital in Boston, said that this work "opens the door for more research on omega-3 fatty acid's effect on a variety of other psychiatric disorders."

Dr. William Connor from Oregon Health Sciences University has been studying omega-3 fats for two decades. He believes that fish oil has more potential for fighting heart disease than aspirin. Although aspirin has repeatedly been found to decrease the risk of blood clots and reduce inflammation in arteries, Dr. Connor has found EPA does the same and more.

Dr. Scott Goodnight also writes, "lab experiments show EPA reduces the amount of thromboxane A2 (a "bad" eicosanoid)." This substance is a potent prostaglandin that promotes blood clotting. EPA loaded cells are able to synthesize other prostaglandins (PGI2 and PGI3) which further act to limit blood clotting. In short, this causes the prostaglandin profile (a list of measurable risk factors) to shift toward a blood consistency that helps prevent strokes and heart attacks.

So what does all this mean as far as diet is concerned? One of the easiest and safest ways to consume enough EPA is to eat at least two fatty fish meals per week. Some scientists also believe that there are other, as yet unidentified substances, in fish fat that promote good health.

So what fish is useful? One of the richest food sources of EPA is red salmon. Dr. William Castelli, director for 16 years of the renowned Framington Heart study, agrees. This study has tracked the cardiovascular health of its subjects in Framington

Massachusetts, since the 1940's. Castelli tells his patients to eat fish at least twice a week, preferably salmon. Salmon contains about 27 times the amount of EPA as, for example, the same amount of sole fish.

And a 1993 study from the Centers for Disease Control and Prevention revealed that Alaskan natives whose main protein source was salmon had fewer than one-third the number of heart attacks as U.S. whites, even though they were twice as likely to be cigarette smokers. Quitting smoking would further decrease their rates of heart attack.

You do not, however, have to run out and buy loads of salmon. There are many other valuable sources of fish, seafood and even supplemental EPA. Eating a wide variety of foods can help ensure optimal vitamin and mineral intake. Variety also decreases the risk of developing food allergies. So how much EPA do we need and what other sources are there, besides salmon?

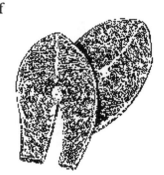

EPA rich salmon

The *New England Journal of Medicine* published a study in 1985 which suggested that 200 mg of EPA per week was enough to significantly cut the risk of heart attacks. The following chart lists several sources of EPA.

SEAFOOD

Common Sources of omega-3 fats

Mackerel	Albacore Tuna
Chinook salmon	Sardines
Striped Bass	Lake Whitefish
Trout	Lobster
Halibut	Sole
Cod	Coho Salmon
Perch	Scallops

Fish should be as fresh as possible. The flesh should glisten, spring back to the touch and be free of any strong fishy odors. However, don't ignore frozen varieties, since the flash freezing methods now in common use can make them an even better nutritional buy than so called "fresh" fish.

People who enjoy seafood will also benefit by using 1-2 teaspoons per day of emulsified cod liver oil. Believe it or not, there are pleasant tasting brands on the market. This is an inexpensive and safe way to tip the balance of EPA in your favor. This suggestion is supported by a 1996 article in the *New England Journal of Medicine* that found fish oil to lessen the symptoms of a variety of illnesses, especially Crohns disease.

Nonetheless, whatever you choose to use, be it a vitamin, mineral, herb, fish oil or anything else, it is wise not to over consume. Back to balance again. Ph.D. dietitian Dr. Barbara Deskins writes that excessive fish oil consumption can cause both internal and external bleeding. Too much fish oil can also cause anemia, so use only 1-2 teaspoons per day. If possible, split the dose between morning and afternoon.

Cholesterol Truth

Most grocery store shelves suggest that cholesterol is the evil villain in human health. Hundreds of products that previously had no connection with cholesterol are shouting about their "cholesterol free" benefits. Even makers of sugar loaded desserts and cereals use these tactics in an effort to sell more products. For example, one cereal maker has a checklist on the front of their package that reads:

- ✔ No cholesterol
- ✔ No fat
- ✔ High fiber
- ✔ Antioxidant rich
- ✔ Added vitamins and minerals

No wonder many believe that cereals are manna from heaven. Unfortunately, this specific product also contains 66 grams of carbohydrate per serving. Apart from some questionable fiber and vitamins, (the type of fiber may even prevent the absorption of nutrients) eating this cereal is little better nutritionally than eating a bowl of sugar. Would a bag of sugar labeled "no cholesterol" encourage you to buy it?

If a previously high cholesterol food is changed in some way to lower or eliminate the cholesterol content, will eating this product contribute to better health? Should we be trying to avoid cholesterol in foods such as shrimp, meat and eggs? Is food cholesterol dangerous?

The truth is that each of us has a genetic tendency to maintain a certain level of cholesterol. Only a small amount comes from the food we eat, while most of it is made in our own liver and gut (intestines). The liver makes the vast majority of cholesterol.

If you eat little cholesterol rich food, then your liver ends up producing more. If you eat a lot of cholesterol, for example, a huge bowl of shrimp, then your liver will make less. Australian endocrinologist, Dr. Martin Sulway, discusses this in his diabetes teaching kit known as Bodylink.

He explains why some people can eat large amounts of cholesterol rich foods, yet have little change occurring in their total cholesterol levels. For most people, cholesterol in food simply doesn't matter. We do know, however, that too much saturated fat *combined with a high carbohydrate diet* can stimulate the liver to overproduce cholesterol.

But is it a worthwhile goal to try and get our cholesterol as low as possible? Clearly not, since cholesterol is essential for human survival. No cholesterol equals no cell structure and no life. A plummeting cholesterol level is also a well-accepted marker for various types of cancer. For example, patients with chronic lymphatic leukemia show diminished blood cholesterol levels.

Physician and author, Dr. Joel Wallach, also believes that the alarming increase in Alzheimer's disease is due to our overemphasis on low cholesterol, low fat diets. His theories seem reasonable when you consider that the human brain is primarily made up of fat and cholesterol.

Cholesterol is also needed for:

1) controlling the flow of nutrients into and out of cells

2) the production of a variety of hormones, including estrogen and testosterone

3) the proper digestion of food, (cholesterol is in bile acids)

4) proper absorption of fat soluble vitamins A, D, E and K

5) growth, development and proper functioning of the nervous system, including the brain

6) the repair of cell damage from injury

7) transporting and balancing blood fats (triglycerides) throughout your body

8) promoting strong immunity to fight infection, cancer and other assaults

So if cholesterol is necessary for health, why is it feared by so many North Americans? There are both good (HDL) and bad (LDL) cholesterol and there are several other sub-classes to these types. Unfortunately, most people tend to focus on total cholesterol rather than the more important ratio of good cholesterol (HDL) to bad cholesterol (LDL)

Physicians Dr. Michael Eades and Dr. Mary Dan Eades write that:

1) your total cholesterol level divided by your HDL cholesterol level should be below four, and

2) your LDL divided by your HDL should be below three

In short, good health requires a certain balance of cholesterol, with more good cholesterol (HDL) and less bad cholesterol (LDL).

Dr. Sulway describes HDL as being like a "Mr. Plumber" since it travels in the blood stream to remove and return excess blood fat to the liver. In contrast LDL picks up blood fats and deposits them in the blood vessels. LDL is not all bad, but it tends to narrow blood vessels and decrease circulation, while HDL tends to open blood vessels and promote blood circulation.

Optimum health has occasionally been described as being equivalent to great circulation. While a strong heart and clear blood vessels may not be a complete definition of health, it is certainly relevant to the prevention of many chronic illnesses. Everything from Type II diabetes, certain cancers and even autoimmune

HDL: the "Mr. Plumber" of cholesterol

disorders are less likely to strike if we have good circulation. We function best and enjoy feeling well when our bloodstream is delivering adequate oxygen and nutrients throughout our entire body.

Consider what happens to cholesterol and circulation if we follow a low fat diet. While it is true that reducing fat can lower total cholesterol levels, doing so also lowers good (HDL) cholesterol. Why do high carbohydrate diets cause a decrease in good cholesterol? Without going into too much detail, the answer lies in understanding a bit about enzymes, insulin and glucagon. Let's look at a simplified version.

The production of cholesterol in the liver is controlled by an enzyme with the tongue twisting name, 3-hydroxy-3-methylglutaryl-coenzyme A reductase. Good grief, let's just call it co-enzyme A. In fact, one of the most popular cholesterol lowering drugs, Lovastatin, acts to inhibit this co-enzyme. Unfortunately, Lovastatin can also cause a range of nasty side effects including serious liver and psychiatric problems, not to mention its hefty cost of over $50 per week, for life.

Fortunately, scientists have proven that insulin acts to stimulate co-enzyme A, thus increasing the production of bad cholesterol. By comparison, insulin's biological opposite, glucagon, inhibits it. Glucagon acts in a similar way to the cholesterol-lowering drug, Lovastatin, but without the cost or negative side effects. In short, insulin increases bad cholesterol, while glucagon limits it.

If we control our intake of carbohydrates, while consuming enough protein and fat, then we naturally move toward a healthier cholesterol level. Unfortunately, many health practitioners still cling to the belief that dietary fat causes high cholesterol. It certainly keeps patients coming back for drugs and doctor visits, but they rarely get better.

Those who remain skeptical of the scientific validity of these ideas are encouraged to read an August, 1997 article from the *New England Journal of Medicine* entitled "Should a low fat, high carbohydrate diet be recommended for everyone?"

This report was authored by some of the worlds leading nutritional scientists, including Dr. W. Willett from Boston, Massachusetts, Dr. S. Grundy from Dallas, Texas and Dr. M. Katan from Wageningen, the Netherlands. The article concludes by doubting the wisdom of recommending low fat diets.

In closing this chapter on dietary fat, let's review three reasons for regularly eating reasonable amounts of fat:

1) Dietary fat has no affect on insulin levels or blood sugar. Both are significant risk factors for obesity, heart disease and cancer.

2) Fat releases the hormone cholecystokinin (CCK), which signals your brain to stop eating. Eating both fat and protein helps curb the appetite and prevent overeating.

3) Fat acts to slow the absorption of glucose into the blood stream. Slower glucose entry causes less insulin secretion. Too much insulin makes us sick and tired.

Part II
Plan to Win

7.

Consider the Evidence

*Eat less, but be sure to have enough
protein, fat, vitamins and minerals.*
Professor Richard Weindruch MD Ph.D.,
longevity researcher,
in *Scientific American.*

Disease Prevention

For years I was amazed at the sheer number of
health problems my patients were experiencing. Although my specialty was obesity and diabetes, I soon

realized that illness rarely occurs in isolation. Arthritis, heart disease, depression, lupus, chronic fatigue, migraines, infections, even cancer and other life threatening conditions often accompany both weight problems and diabetes.

In fact, it is not surprising that sick people typically suffer from not one, but several different health complaints. Chronic ill health often results from a persistently weak immune system (defense system). The specific disorder that weak immunity allows to attack us will depend on genetic and environmental circumstances. Having strong immunity, however, is no guarantee of protection from potent viruses, bacteria, poisons or other assaults. Yet these are rare dangers that make up only a fraction of a percent of all illnesses.

Immune Support

High insulin (hyperinsulinemia) is well known to depress immunity. Authors Dr. Michael Eades and Dr. Mary Dan Eades have described it as a "monster hormone," and anyone familiar with diabetes will understand this description. Excess insulin has a profound affect on increasing a variety of "bad" eicosanoid hormones.

As you now know, these master hormones affect virtually every aspect of human physiology. New research has shown that eicosanoids influence pain transmission, inflammation, blood clotting, immunity, blood vessel size, fertility, cancer and more. Some of the well-known "bad" eicosanoids include certain types of prostaglandins, leukotrines, thromboxanes and others.

High insulin levels have been scientifically linked to well over 33 different health complaints. A Medline computer search of over 10 years' accumulated research revealed at least one, and in some cases dozens of research papers connecting high insulin levels with:

- Type II Diabetes
- Heart Disease
- Obesity
- Depression
- Arthritis
- Osteoporosis
- Cancer
- Sleep Disorders
- Headaches
- Eating Disorders
- Infertility / PMS
- Sinus Problems
- Infections
- Menopause Symptoms
- Poor Athleticism
- Chronic Hunger

- Chronic Fatigue
- Blood Pressure
- Respiratory Failure
- Gall Stones
- Cushings disease
- Kidney Disease
- Retinopathy (eyes)
- Polycystic Ovaries
- Lupus
- Multiple Sclerosis
- Mood disorders
- Brittle Hair & Nails
- Fluid Retention
- Constipation
- Vaginal Infections
- Temperature Intolerance

Although the previous list is long and may seem surprising, it is really just the tip of the iceberg. Since all parts of the human body are intimately connected, a weakening in one system will inevitably affect the whole. Many factors can tip the balance of good health, but food intake is one of the most powerful ways to regain control.

Unifying Factors

One of the major flaws of most health advice is that it is fragmented and incomplete. We hear little bits of information, yet we fail to put all the puzzle pieces into a single picture. We see articles with titles like "Vitamin E Magic" or "Success through Meditation" or "The Antioxidant Cure." Such publicity can provide useful but incomplete information. As a wise physician once said "everyone is a little bit right."

The challenge in science is to find some unifying factors that help us to understand the entire picture. Insulin balance is undoubtedly important to well-being and longevity. After all, the three master keys to health are diet, moderate exercise and stress reduction, and all play powerful roles in limiting insulin.

Of course stress reduction can include such things as meditation, confiding in friends, walking, yoga, massage, and much more. Even universal spiritual laws such as forgiveness, love, prayer, and self-acceptance can measurably prevent the harmful release of stress hormones such as adrenaline and cortisol. Too much adrenaline and cortisol in our blood stream causes blood glucose (sugar) to rise. And when blood glucose rises, so too does insulin.

And even the placebo effect (you think it will work and so it does) can lower the amount of insulin being produced. The mere act of believing in some benign treatment can put our mind at such ease as to lower adrenaline, cortisol and insulin.

Confiding Friendships

Harvard physician, Dr. Herbert Benson, coined the term "the relaxation response" to describe the profound health benefits experienced by regularly eliciting this particular state of calm.

In addition, having a definite purpose in life helps us avoid such dangers as worrying, self-reproach, blaming and other negative thought patterns. When our lives have meaning, we are less likely to overeat or abuse alcohol or other drugs. Believing in our abilities and pursuing our dreams has several benefits, one of which, surprise, surprise, is to control insulin.

Furthermore, while moderate exercise lowers this hormone, overly strenuous exercise (we're talking several hours of really sweating) can cause the release of stress hormones that raise insulin. Excessive perspiration also causes the loss of essential minerals, which unless replaced, can be harmful. Still, the majority of people need more activity, not less.

So when it comes to health advice, everyone may be a little correct, but one unifying factor is clearly related to the biochemical control of insulin. Understand the factors that control this hormone and you understand how to promote better health.

Specific Disease States

While it is beyond the scope of this book to detail all the evidence in support of our dietary suggestions, the following section provides important and relevant findings. No one finding is meant to stand alone as conclusive proof. Rather, these are written as reinforcement for the overall view of how food intake and insulin levels affect our health.

Diabetes and Heart Disease

> *Our data are incompatible with the view that dietary fat intake has any causal role in cardiovascular health.*
>
> (*Social Science and Medicine*, August, 1994)

As mentioned previously, diabetes is closely linked to many disorders, especially heart disease. Although heart disease can occur alone, most people with poorly controlled diabetes have some form 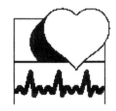 of heart damage. They are also at increased risk of suffering from heart attacks and strokes.

The common factor for all people with newly diagnosed diabetes is that they have a high blood sugar level. In fact, doctors refer to pre-diabetes as glucose intolerance. Isn't it strange that conventional dietary wisdom treats people who are glucose intolerant by telling them to consume high glucose producing diets? Recommending carbohydrates to people with diabetes is like encouraging milk consumption to those with lactose (milk sugar) intolerance. It makes no sense.

Of all people with diabetes, about 90% have the Type II condition. Of these, most suffer from high blood pressure, weight problems, insulin resistance, high triglycerides and excess LDL (bad) cholesterol. People with diabetes also suffer from a higher incidence of depression, arthritis, cancer, eating disorders and even alcoholism.

Meanwhile, media food messages tend to emphasize the supposed dangers of eating both fat and cholesterol. Yet a 1996 article published in the *Social Science and Medicine Journal* states that "the low fat, low cholesterol diet was ill-conceived from the outset and, with the accumulation of new evidence, it is becoming increasingly less tenable."

In addition, a 1996 study published in the *International Journal of Epidemiology* reveals that "Mediterranean regions with the lowest consumption of total and saturated fats register the highest mortality due to heart disease." Regular wine and fish consumption also helped to explain the paradox of less heart disease in those who ate plenty of fat.

Similarly, an early study from a 1983 article published in the journal *Medical Hypotheses* concluded:

> Evidence from diet and drug intervention studies support the hypothesis that dietary lipid (fat) is only of secondary importance in coronary heart disease. Refined carbohydrates are of primary importance.

Yet our understanding of sugar speed (glycemic index) makes the term "refined carbohydrates" somewhat meaningless. It is high glycemic carbohydrates, or the ones that are most rapidly turned into blood glucose, that create problems. These include such things as potatoes, pasta, bread, and juices.

As well, a 1995 study in the *Journal of the American Dietetic Association* looked at the impact of meat consumption on cardiovascular risk factors in young adults. They concluded, "consumption of moderate amounts of lean meat, along with healthier choices in other food groups, may be necessary to meet current dietary recommendations."

There are also benefits to regularly eating small amounts of fruit. This idea is supported by a 1996 study published in The *British Medical Journal* which found that daily consumption of fresh fruit was associated with reduced mortality from ischaemic heart disease, cerebrovascular disease and all causes combined.

And finally, as far as diabetes and heart disease is concerned, there is much evidence to support the benefits of fish oil. An April 1998 article published in the prestigious journal *Diabetes Care* states that "The use of fish oil in diabetic subjects lowers triglyceride levels by almost 30%." They conclude, "Fish oil may be useful in treating dyslipidemia in diabetics."

Infections

Have you ever noticed that you end up getting a cold or flu during or after emotional distress? As mentioned previously, stress causes the release of cortisol and adrenaline. These, in turn, increase insulin, which then depresses immunity. A weak immune system makes you more vulnerable to illness and infection.

In addition, anyone who has worked with diabetes patients knows that high blood sugar delays wound healing and increases the risk of infection. A classic example is the diabetic leg ulcer, which may require months of hospitalization. Simply lowering blood sugar and insulin will quickly help to heal these wounds.

Furthermore, studies looking at a type of fungus that causes female yeast infections, called candida albicans, have shown that it fails to grow unless supplemented with sugar. Similarly, a report looking at 100 women with recurring vaginal yeast infections found increased infection with high carbohydrate intake.

Impotence

Ask any diabetes physician about the relationship between high blood glucose and male sexuality and they will tell you that men with chronically elevated blood sugar levels also suffer from high rates of impotence. In fact, it has been estimated that over 50% of these men are unable to have an erection. Controlling blood sugar levels can prevent this. Unfortunately, doing so is almost impossible to achieve on a carbohydrate-loaded diet.

Consider too, that one of the most common treatments for erectile dysfunction is the injection of PGE1 (a good eicosanoid) directly into the penis. Unfortunately, most men are not too thrilled about sticking sharp objects into tender parts of their anatomy. It is far better to understand how food can solve the problem. Taking the right dietary action will not only prevent impotence; it will improve other aspects of health.

On the other hand, a drug called Viagra is becoming a popular treatment for impotence. These pills, however, have recently been linked to several serious side affects, including heart attack and death.

No single drug is ever the answer when it comes to promoting health. Medications typically attack the symptoms of illness but do little or nothing to cure the underlying *cause* of the problem. The human body is too complex for a single bullet approach.

Depression / Mental Alertness

Have North Americans suddenly given birth to a new generation of Prozac or Zoloft deficient babies? If not, then what is the explanation for the almost epidemic rise in cases of clinical depression? Evidence suggests that conventional dietary guidelines are contributing to poor mental health.

For example, women suffer far greater rates of depression than men. They also tend to be more interested in listening to media based food fads. Women are more likely to diet by avoiding fat and this means reducing the intake of meat and dairy products (and therefore, protein). They may also believe that avoiding fat will make them thin.

A 1996 study published in the International *Journal of Eating Disorders* found that "non-depressed subjects consumed more protein and depressed subjects consumed more carbohydrates." The authors concluded that:

Increased carbohydrate consumption is consistent with the carbohydrate cravings characteristic of the depressed and may relate to the development or maintenance of depression.

Several other studies have linked low fat and low cholesterol diets to higher rates of depression and suicide. For example, Dr. Joseph Hibbeln, a psychiatrist at the National Institute of Alcohol Abuse and Alcoholism, believes that the amount of omega-3 fish fat relative to the amount of omega-6 fat is a critical factor in mental health. He says that too much omega-6 combined with too little omega-3 increases the risks for depression.

In countries such as Taiwan and Japan where people eat high amounts of fish, the depression rate runs 10 times lower than in North America. Depression is a complex disorder, but dietary modification can make a positive difference. Author, Dr. Michael Nordon, is among the many psychiatrists who have successfully used dietary changes for treating depression.

Is there other evidence to link insulin with mental stability? We know that exercise lowers insulin, but it is not a universal cure for depression. However, results of several studies, including a 1993 write up in the *Journal of Psychosomatic Research* shows that exercise programs do have anti-depressant, anti-anxiety and mood enhancing effects.

Exercise acts to lower blood insulin levels for up to 36 hours after exercise is stopped. This is believed to occur due to an increased sensitivity of insulin receptor sites. Increased sensitivity results in more insulin being removed from the blood stream and taken up by the fat and muscle cells.

The inconsistency in the success rate of exercise as a cure for depression probably lies in the lack of simultaneous attention to nutrient intake and other factors, such as psychotherapy. The ideal exercise routine won't cure depression in a person who eats a nutrient deficient, high carbohydrate diet or has unresolved psychological issues.

Eating Disorders

Eating disorders are invariably linked to depression. It is difficult to know which comes first, but depressed mood can certainly initiate an eating disorder. Inadequate nutrition then acts to sustain poor mental health. Depression has already been discussed, so what other evidence is there to link conventional dietary advice to eating disorders?

Avoidance of fat can cause serious changes in appetite and behavior. People pleasing or perfection driven women (and some men) can begin dangerous eating disorders with ultra low fat diets. Following such regimes is difficult and most people cannot continue. The result is guilt, self-loathing and binge/purge (overeating and vomitting) behaviors.

A 1995 study in the journal *Addictive Behaviors* found binge prone women to be more depressed, have lower self-esteem, and have more chaotic and extreme eating patterns than those with normal eating habits. Advertising images of thin, flawless looking women also contribute to unrealistic expectations and destructive thought patterns.

Recovery from eating disorders involves restoring a healthy biochemical balance and learning how to replace destructive thought patterns with more effective ways of thinking. Being aware of our environment and consciously choosing to read, look at, and listen to positive messages has the power to promote health. Chapter nine expands on this topic.

Alcoholism

Evidence suggests that both depressives and alcoholics have a genetic defect in the ability to make an essential fat called gamma linoleic acid (GLA). Controlled studies have found alcoholics to have as little as half the blood level of GLA compared to normal people. Well-documented biochemical steps show that this low GLA level results in a decreased ability to make good eicosanoids.

On the other hand, moderate alcohol consumption temporarily raises the level of good eicosanoids, which helps people feel better. Limited amounts of alcohol can also give a temporary boost to the cardiovascular system. This is not intended to encourage alcohol consumption, but if you choose to indulge, do so while eating and restrict your intake to 1–2 glasses of wine, beer or dry spirits per day.

The down side to drinking, for those with a genetic defect in making GLA, is that their "feel good" reaction is typically short lived. Alcoholics end up needing more and more alcohol just to feel normal. Drinking large amounts of alcohol is well known to be dangerous. So what can be done to raise the level of GLA and thus curb the desire for alcohol?

GLA is contained in whole oats and slow cooking oatmeal. A small daily serving can be useful, but simply following our protein to carbohydrate ratios will naturally increase the enzyme needed to change linoleic acid into GLA. The correct protein to carbohydrate ratio acts to significantly curb the craving for alcohol.

Low dose GLA supplements can also help. A series of 1984 trials conducted by Dr. Ian Glen showed that GLA supplements significantly reduced the craving for alcohol. GLA supplements include such things as evening primrose and borage oil. Unfortunately, many of these over-the-counter supplements have been shown to contain very little GLA. Try following our food guidelines first. If you still feel a need to supplement, then purchase a product from a reputable company.

Chronic Fatigue Syndrome

Chronic fatigue syndrome is a debilitating and poorly understood illness. It was almost unheard of prior to the North American obsession with avoiding dietary fat. We also know that one's susceptibility and outcome from chronic fatigue syndrome is closely tied to immune strength.

Scientists believe that eicosanoid balance plays a key role in protecting us from this debilitating syndrome. For example, Dr. J.B. Gray and Dr. A.M. Martinovic published a study entitled "Eicosanoid and Essential Fatty Acid Modulation in Chronic Disease and Chronic Fatigue Syndrome." They were the first to explain how chronically lowered immunity, triggered by a low intake of essential fatty acids, leads to this condition.

Their interventions were remarkably successful. Over 90% of their subjects gained significant improvement within three months and more than two-thirds became fit enough to return to full time duties. These results came from simply improving the balance of dietary essential fatty acids. Sufficient intake of magnesium has also been found to improve chronic fatigue syndrome.

As well, there is good reason to believe that our recommendations can make a positive difference in general levels of fatigue. Excess carbohydrates have repeatedly been implicated in contributing to fatigue. For example, a 1989 study published in The *Journal of Clinical Psychiatry* looked at the composition of three different meals (repeat occasions) and found that even when given the same number of calories, women consuming high carbohydrate meals had significantly increased feelings of fatigue.

Test this hypothesis for yourself. Keep track of your fatigue about 2-3 hours after a protein adequate, low carbohydrate lunch compared to a high carbohydrate meal. Consume the same number of calories and assess your response on different occasions. All else being equal, people feel more tired after consuming excess carbohydrate. Be sure to exclude periods of inadequate sleep, high stress or caffeine use that would affect results.

Fatigue

Pre-Menstrual Syndrome (PMS)

Several studies have linked poor nutrition with increased severity of premenstrual symptoms. For example, a 1991 study published in the *Journal of Reproductive Medicine* looked at 853 female university students and found that high dietary sugar content was significantly associated with the prevalence of premenstrual syndrome.

Similarly, a 1982 article in the *Journal of Applied Nutrition* found that women who reported symptoms of premenstrual syndrome consumed significantly higher amounts of refined carbohydrates. Once again, being aware of sugar speed is more useful than talking about "refined carbohydrates." Low sugar speed foods are preferred since they tend to be high in nutrients and are slow to turn into blood glucose.

High sugar speed carbohydrates increase insulin secretion. Insulin acts to suppress important substances known as ketoacids. Since ketoacids help the kidney clear excess sodium and water, insufficient amounts cause water retention (bloating) and worsening of PMS symptoms.

Excess carbohydrate also increases the urinary excretion of magnesium, a deficiency of which has been shown to contribute to PMS. Authors of a 1986 report published in the *Annals of Clinical Biochemistry* wrote, "We have tested many disorders and PMS is the only one that is correlated with lower than normal levels of magnesium." The recommended adult intake for magnesium is between 300–400 mg per day. Good food sources of this mineral are listed in the following chart.

Magnesium Rich Foods Include:

- Soy Flour
- Soybeans
- Tofu
- Broccoli
- Spinach
- Beet greens
- Cashews

- Lima beans
- Brazil nuts
- Pecans
- Peanuts
- Walnuts
- Avocados
- Oatmeal

Dietary fat is also related to PMS. For example, excessive menstrual pain in Danish women has been correlated with low omega-3 fat intake. A study published in the July 1995 *European Journal of Clinical Nutrition* investigated the menstrual pain of 181 women aged 20 - 45. This study found that a low intake of both animal and fish products correlated with increased menstrual pain. The average dietary omega-3 to omega-6 ratio for women with menstrual pain was a low 0.24. The authors concluded that "The results were highly significant and supported the hypothesis that a higher intake of marine fatty acids (fish fat) correlates with milder menstrual symptoms."

Women who consume plenty of caffeine are also more likely to suffer from PMS. Caffeine stimulates gluconeogenesis (release of glucose from the liver), which promotes insulin release. Caffeine also increases the level of bad cholesterol (LDL). Giving up coffee or tea is easy once you understand how food alone can boost and sustain your energy levels.

If you suffer from PMS or painful menstrual cramps you will also benefit from light weight lifting. Although walking, cycling and other aerobic activities have *not* been found to relieve cramps, weight lifting has. It releases powerful enzymes into the blood stream that quickly and dramatically ease menstrual pain. Learn how to lift slowly, with the correct position, and you will be amazed with the results. It may be the last thing you feel like doing, but it works.

Fertility

Think of fertility and most people think of hormones. Indeed, the human reproductive cycle is closely tied to a delicate balance of several important hormones such as estrogen, test-osterone, progesterone, and yes, even insulin. As a fat storage hormone, insulin is intimately linked to both obesity, at one extreme, and being too thin at the other end of the spectrum.

Severe weight loss will result in lack of menstruation and infertility. Obesity also dampens the essential reproductive hormones. Back to balance again.

Obesity and excess insulin can also negatively alter the balance of eicosanoids known as prostaglandins. A poor prostaglandin profile contributes to endometriosis, a common cause of infertility. For example, a January 1994 study published in the International *Journal of Fertility and Menopausal Studies* investigated the role of prostaglandins and tubal function in endometriosis. The authors concluded that patients with endometriosis produced more PGE and PGF (bad eicosanoids) than did normal control subjects.

In addition, a condition of abnormal cell growth on ovaries, known as polycystic ovary disease is strongly linked to infertility. Women with this condition invariably have higher than normal insulin levels.

Dietary fats play an important role in reproductive health. For example, studies have demonstrated that low fat diets diminish fertility in lab animals. There is also an association between the ratio of omega-3 and omega-6 fatty acids and ovulation. Low omega-3 fat intake can disrupt normal ovulation and lead to infertility.

A 1995 animal study published in the journal of *Reproduction and Fertility* looked at different intakes of n-3 to n-6 fatty acids. They found that "incorporation of n-3 fatty acids appeared to enhance ovulation." The authors concluded, "dietary lipids affect ovulation in rats, with possible implications for reproduction in other vertebrates."

Menopause

Aging for both men and women typically involves predictable changes in a variety of health measures. These include such things as fasting blood glucose, LDL cholesterol, blood pressure, triglycerides and others. Yet the most significant rise is seen in blood insulin levels. Evidence suggests that this is especially true for women who suffer from hot flashes, sleep disturbances, depression and irritability.

You don't need a Ph.D. in Public Health to realize that the high carbohydrate, low fat diet is a big failure for menopausal women. Simply look at the dramatic rise in obesity, heart disease, diabetes and depression in this age group.

A Toronto food seminar on the topic of hormones and depression recently drew a middle-aged crowd of over 700 mainly overweight, depressed looking women. Such a large response suggests that conventional dietary advice has not yet provided the correct answers. After all, this seminar was targeted at health professionals who are well aware of standard dietary guidelines. These guidelines don't work.

Unfortunately, the main message from the registered dietitian giving the presentation merely echoed the tired old refrain about "eating a low fat, high carbohydrate diet." If we keep believing what we've been believing, we'll keep achieving what we've been achieving.

There is sound evidence to support abolishing the low fat, high carbohydrate diet, especially for postmenopausal women. One of the most convincing studies is entitled, "Effects of Low-Fat, High Carbohydrate Diets on Risk Factors for Ischemic Heart Disease in Postmenopausal Women." This 1997 trial was published in the *American Journal of Clinical Nutrition*. It came from the department of medicine at Stanford University.

Results from this hospital based study showed that postmenopausal women who follow a lower carbohydrate, higher fat diet had significantly better measures of cardiac health than did women on high carbohydrate, low fat diets. The authors concluded, "it seems reasonable to question the wisdom of recommending that post menopausal women consume low-fat, high carbohydrate diets."

Such findings are of great significance for our collective well-being. The health of millions of women either entering or just beyond menopause can influence economic and social factors in our society. The power of nutrition has wide-ranging implications.

Unfortunately, it is difficult to overcome advertising messages from powerful food companies that make everything from sports drinks and cereal to cookies and "diet" rice cakes. Such foods have an exceptionally high sugar speed and do not promote good health. Top this off with endorsements from national health associations who also want a financial cut and it is little wonder that people are confused.

Cancer

The U.S. National Academy of Sciences estimates that 60% of female cancers and 40% of male cancers are related to nutrition. Other scientists believe this to be an understatement. In any case, we know that dietary habits certainly influence your chances of getting, and perhaps dying, from cancer.

The past 50 years of medical research has also developed a strong link between obesity and many types of cancer. And of course, high levels of blood insulin are typically seen with obesity. Excess insulin contributes to a variety of different cancers. Control insulin, while eating enough essential nutrients and you will reduce your cancer risk. But there's more to the picture.

Media messages make us believe that saturated fat is the cancer villain, but not a single study has shown that high fat, low carbohydrate diets cause this condition. Indeed, the head of nutrition at Harvard, Dr. Walter Willett, recently said that dietary fat has been given far too much blame when it comes to cancer.

A November 1995 study in the journal *Cancer Causes and Control* looked at over 2500 people living in various parts of Italy and found that the regular consumption of olive oil had an inverse relationship to breast cancer. In other words, regular use of olive oil decreased ones risk of getting breast cancer.

Omega-3 fish fat also plays a valuable role in prevention. For example, a November 1995 study published in the Journal *Oncology* found that EPA and DHA from fish oils showed significant anti breast cancer activity. In fact, use of EPA in animal experiments has consistently been shown to improve health and longevity.

And what about the carbohydrate link to cancer? A 1996 study published in the European *Journal of Cancer Prevention*, showed that the strongest association with reduction in cancer deaths was related to the consumption of green vegetables. Remember that it is difficult to over consume carbohydrates in the form of green vegetables.

Another example in support of fruit and vegetable consumption appeared in a 1996 study published in the *Journal of the Royal Society of Health*. They found that regular consumption of both fruit and vegetables was consistently associated with a lower risk of cancer, especially of the digestive and respiratory tract.

Few people dispute the health value of eating fruits and vegetables, but it is usually vitamins and minerals that are seen to be of most benefit. Fruits and vegetables contain more vitamins and minerals than pasta and bagels. However, the more significant value of fibrous vegetables lies in their ability to control insulin.

An April 1992 study published in the *International Journal of Cancer* found that gastric cancer risk increased with increasing sugar, meal and flour products, including white bread. The same study found that consumption of lean meat was associated with a decreased risk of gastric cancer.

Now what about the notion that pollutants in our environment cause cancer? Breathing fresh air and drinking clean water are desirable objectives and environment does influence health. How much cancer causing blame should be assigned to pollution?

It may feel right to emotionally point an accusatory finger at a dirty environment, but there is little to support this belief. For example, one of the most convincing studies showing that pesticides do *not* cause cancer comes from Harvard Medical School. This ongoing study of several thousand nurses was published in the *New England Journal of Medicine*. Ironically, women with the highest levels of pesticide residues in their blood actually have a *lower* risk of getting breast cancer. Perhaps this group simply kept insulin levels low by incidentally eating more pesticide-laden fruits and vegetables.

Moreover, the Harvard results serve to confirm what other investigators have found. For example, Dr. Pamela Goodwin from the Marvell Koffler Breast Center at Toronto's Mount Sinai Hospital says, "There is no association between breast cancer and the most common environmental chemicals such as DDT and PCB's that are routinely blamed for causing cancer."

In addition, Dr. Stephen Safe, a toxicologist at Texas A&M University calls all the hoopla about cancer and the environment "paparazzi science." He notes that studies done in San Francisco, Buffalo, and the European Community have also found no increased levels of pesticides in women with breast cancer. Unfortunately, many people remain attracted to the chemophobia and enviroscare messages spread by the scientifically naive. More enlightened researchers are now turning to diet as the main cause of cancer.

Several types of cancers have been linked to insulin and obesity. It is therefore no surprise to see the results of an ongoing Harvard study of over 95,000 women. This work showed that after 16 years, women who gain 44 to 55 pounds after age 18 are at a 40% higher risk of developing breast cancer after menopause than women who gained only 4–5 pounds in adulthood. Dr. Zhiping Huang led this investigation.

Few people understand the connection between insulin and malignant tumors. Dr. S. Seely and Dr. D Horrobin state in a 1983 M*edical Hypotheses Journal*, that "insulin is an absolute requirement for the proliferation of mammary (breast) tissue and experimental mammary tumors regress in its absence." They go on to write that the same mechanism might account for the increased risk of mammary cancer in women with Type II diabetes.

As well, what do we know about the causes of male prostate cancer? The incidence of prostate cancer has been rising dramatically in the past ten years. Is there any link between obesity, insulin, and this common killer? An August 1984 study published in the *American Journal of Epidemiology* found that "overweight men had a significantly higher risk of fatal prostate cancer than men near their desirable weight." The regular consumption of fresh tomatoes, rich in substances called lycopenes, has also been linked to a decrease risk of prostate cancer.

Unfortunately, not all fruit or vegetable products promote good health. For example, an expensive advertisement supported by juice producers and The American Cancer Society, recently appeared in a popular magazine. It encourages people to believe that drinking large (not small) glasses of juice will supposedly help reduce cancer risks. Yet one of the first things any weight loss dietitian will suggest to their patients is to eat whole fruit instead of drinking juice. This is because fruit and even vegetable juices are high in easily consumable sugar and calories.

Juice, or any high carbohydrate liquid raises blood glucose and insulin levels faster than whole fruit. Drinking juice is better than drinking cola or other zero value soft drinks, but nutrients are better obtained from eating solid foods. Regularly drinking large glasses of juice is no way to avoid excess insulin, obesity or cancer.

Pain

Everyone knows a little about pain, but few understand what causes it. Most of us simply reach for the aspirin bottle or 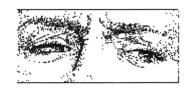 other medication. But pills offer only temporary *symptomatic* relief. Excessive or prolonged use of drugs is not the solution. So what are two of the main causes of pain and what can be done about them?

The first and most common cause of discomfort is from mechanical damage, such as rubbing, pinching, burning or other physical injury or pressure on nerve fibers. Getting rid of the source of irritation provides relief for this kind of pain. Chiropractic, massage therapy, physiotherapy, acupuncture, exercise, and, as a last resort, surgery, have all been successful in eliminating mechanical pain.

However, as any headache or arthritis sufferer can confirm, there are also biochemical causes of pain. Biochemical pain messengers send powerful signals to our brain telling us that something is wrong. Pharmaceutical scientists have known for decades that the biochemical causes of pain are due to an overproduction of bad eicosanoids. These eicosanoids include such things as PGE2 and Leukotriene B4, whereas one of the good eicosanoids, PGE1 acts to block the release of other pain causing chemicals.

Lower insulin levels and you naturally increase the good PGE1 hormones while putting the brakes on the overproduction of bad eicosanoids. Precise laboratory measurements of potential pain relieving formulas are repeatedly tested to see how they affect these master hormones. The 1982 Nobel prize in Medicine was awarded for work which explained how aspirin works to alter a subclass of eicosanoids known as prostaglandins.

It was found that aspirin decreases the level of PGE1. Unfortunately, long term use of aspirin can result in gastric bleeding and even death. Likewise, excessive use of other common pain relievers can cause kidney failure, while popular anti-inflammatory drugs lower immune function and damage your liver.

All of these over-the-counter pain relievers knock out PGE1, but they have no affect on other bad eicosanoids, such as leukotrienes. To block these, you need stronger prescription drugs such as cortisone and prednisone. Unfortunately, these drugs lower your resistence to infection and increase your risk of getting all kinds of diseases. These potent drugs also speed the loss of minerals from your bones and contribute to osteoporosis.

So prevention is better than cure, and one of the best pain blocking habits is to follow a protein and fat adequate, low carbohydrate diet. The food guidelines in this book will tip the biochemical balance of pain messengers in your favor. If you understand how food, stress management and moderate activity control insulin levels, then you can act to dampen the most common causes of aches and pains.

This doesn't mean that food can cure all pain. Pain relieving drugs will always play a role in curbing human misery. Sudden injury, burns, care of the dying and other situations often require pharmaceutical intervention. Yet whenever possible, the path of prevention is the best solution. Food is the safest baseline therapy for reducing the risk of long term dependence on pain medication.

Arthritis

Think of arthritis and you naturally think of pain. Since the previous section has already covered some of the biochemical causes of pain, lets look at further evidence to support our dietary interventions for treating arthritis.

Adequate amounts of omega-3 fatty acids will reduce discomfort from arthritis. One of many studies supporting this claim was a controlled, double blind trial published in the October 1992 *Journal of Rheumatology*. The researchers concluded, "significant relief from the symptoms of rheumatoid arthritis could be achieved with dietary omega-3 fatty acid supplementation."

A study published in the May 1996 edition of *Epidemiology* looked at 324 women with rheumatoid arthritis compared to 1245 control subjects who were free from disease. It was found that eating two servings of fish per week was significantly associated with a decreased risk of rheumatoid arthritis. The authors concluded, "These results support the hypothesis that omega-3 fatty acids may help prevent rheumatoid arthritis." You can choose to eat fish twice a week or take small amounts of fish oil supplements.

Even a conservative report from the Scientific Review Committee of Health Canada and similar American publications emphasize the importance of obtaining sufficient amounts of omega-3 fats. The average North American consumption of this type of fat is too low.

Arthritis sufferers have also experienced pain relief by simply consuming small daily amounts of ground up chicken cartilage. What's so special about chicken cartilage? It contains many of the raw materials needed to rebuild human connective tissue, including glucosamine sulphate, collagen and other substances.

There are over a dozen clinical trials showing that glucasamine sulphate can help arthritis sufferers. Moreover, negative side effects are unheard of.

Glucosamine sulphate use has been promoted in many best selling books including *Pain Free and The Arthritis Cure.*

Similarly, vitamin, mineral and trace mineral intake has been associated with the occurrence and progression of arthritis. For example, a large scale study in the June 1996 edition of the *Journal of Rheumatology* found that patients with rheumatoid arthritis typically follow diets that lack sufficient amounts of pyridoxine, zinc, magnesium, copper and folate.

Any good nutrition textbook will reveal that the foods emphasized in our dietary guidelines are exceptionally rich in these micronutrients. So there is reason to believe that our suggestions will prevent or at least reduce arthritis symptoms.

Osteoporosis

Some people hold the mistaken belief that eating a protein adequate diet somehow contributes to osteoporosis. This book outlines a mineral and nutrient rich program that promotes the formation of healthy bones and teeth. It encourages people to consume an adequate amount of protein, depending on lean body mass and activity level.

In addition, the July 1996 *Osteoporosis SOGC Journal Supplement* states "protein supplements may actually be beneficial to the bones, as poor nutrition, particularly poor protein nutrition, carries a significant risk for fracture."

Bone specialist, Dr. R. P. Heaney in a 1993 edition of the *Annual Review of Nutrition* gives the same opinion. The most convincing evidence in support of adequate protein intake to prevent osteoporosis comes from an article entitled "Protein Depletion and Metabolic Stress in Elderly Patients who have a Fracture of the Hip." This study reveals the benefits of adequate protein intake. It was published in a 1992 edition of the journal *Bone & Joint Surgeons of America.*

So regular protein consumption at appropriate time intervals makes good health sense. The danger lies in habitually downing such things as a 2-pound T-bone steak. Gluttony of any kind is risky and eating too much protein at one sitting is just as bad as eating too much carbohydrate or fat. Back to balance again.

Women who want to prevent or even reverse osteoporosis would also benefit by learning more about natural progesterone therapy. Regular use of certain progesterone creams will help you sleep better, build bone, improve hair and skin condition and even renew your sex drive. And while estrogen is well known to increase the risk of cancer, progesterone has no negative side effects.

If you are skeptical of these or other claims for natural progesterone then you may wish to read Dr. John R. Lee's book entitled, *What You're Doctor May Not Tell You About Menopause.* Dr. Lee is a 70-year-old physician with compelling scientific evidence for the benefits of *natural* progesterone. He has shown that bone density in women can be significantly increased by the simple use of this plant based hormone cream. Obstetrician, gynecologist and author Dr. Christiane Northrup shares a similar opinion.

Asthma

A report by Harvard Medical School in Boston, which tracked 100,000 American nurses for over five years, has linked asthma to obesity. The researchers found that women who were obese from the beginning of the study were three times more likely 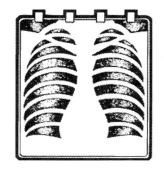 to develop asthma compared to those who were not overweight.

Dr. Carlos Camargo, who led the Harvard study, said that research had not previously looked at the link between asthma and obesity. Some scientists believe that extra weight somehow compresses the airways, yet it is reasonable to believe that an imbalance of eicosanoids is a source of the problem. There are specific eicosanoids that are well known to increase both inflammation and irritation. These unpleasant reactions can occur anywhere in the human body, including the membrane lining of the lungs.

Furthermore, a British study from the United Medical and Dental Schools found that heavy adults were 80% more likely to have asthma than slim ones. Both this study and the Harvard Nurses study were presented at the 1998 International Conference of the American Lung Association and the American Thoracic Society.

Consider as well that the typical asthma sufferer finds it difficult to engage in regular physical activity. Those with asthma symptoms will naturally avoid exercise and continue to miss out on the benefits of this insulin lowering activity.

Lowering insulin decreases the level of specific eicosanoids that promote inflammation and irritation. Asthma, however, like many chronic disease states, is made better or worse by a variety of interventions. Medications may still be necessary but our food guidelines can serve as the ideal baseline therapy for asthma.

Multiple Sclerosis / Cushings / Lupus

Multiple sclerosis (MS) is a potentially tragic condition involving destruction of the myelin covering of nerve fibers. The disease can result in slow and sometimes complete paralysis, as well as psychological impairment. Fortunately, most people experience either short or long-term periods of time when they are completely symptom free.

Since the natural course of the disease is unpredictable, it is impossible to prove exactly what lifestyle changes are helpful. Nonetheless, diet is known to affect the immune system and therefore has an influence over this condition. Furthermore, there have been hundreds of individual, albeit anecdotal, success stories about dietary treatment for Multiple Sclerosis.

For example, one of the more interesting accounts appeared in a 1994 edition of the *Journal of Clinical Epidemiology*. The author, a patient of a neurologist from Yale university, wrote about her "miraculous cure" following 28 years with MS. She went from "being unable to climb onto a doctors table" to "living on my own, driving a Peugeot and teaching junior high." In addition she wrote, "everyday I see that my intestines are working as they never have before, cleaning out wastes, instead of poisoning my system."

And what does this woman eat? She follows a diet designed by a French physician and author named Dr. Catherine Kousmine. Her recommendations emphasize reasonable amounts of easily absorbed, high quality protein, essential fatty acids (mainly monounsaturates), fruit, vegetables, nuts, and limited amounts of whole grain. Sound familiar?

In addition, the March 1997 Ontario edition of the Multiple Sclerosis Society of Canada newsletter provides further evidence in support of the dietary suggestions in this book. It lists a number of potential MS drugs that have been used to fight both arthritis and cancer. These drugs are known to *act directly on eicosanoid balance* and have "immune system modulating and anti-inflammatory effects." One medication was even described as "an anti-cancer drug which can suppress the misguided immune activity in multiple sclerosis."

Unfortunately, the newsletter fails to mention the potentially dangerous side effects of such drugs. The appropriate use of nutrient dense foods, in the right protein to carbohydrate ratio will reduce inflammation and improve immune function, with no adverse side effects.

MS is not the only serious chronic illness that is related to food and insulin. For example, a 1994 study published in *Baillieres Clinical Endocrinology and Metabolism* states "Many of these changes (related to obesity) are also seen in subjects with cushings and polycystic ovary syndrome, *in particular hyperinsulinemia*" (high insulin). Similarly, a June 1995 article published in the *Journal of Autoimmunity* found that dietary omega-3 fats delayed the onset and progression of the common and serious disease known as Lupus.

Conventional medicine typically has no cure for many chronic and degenerative illnesses. Historically, our sad tradition has been to place these people in long term and often hopeless chronic care facilities. Nurses in such institutions spend the majority of their time dispensing questionably effective medications. Better nutrition could at least diminish the need for these drugs.

Skin and Hair Problems

The North American obsession with avoiding fat has lead to an increased incidence of skin and hair problems. While the actual thickness of hair is largely inherited, the health and appearance of skin and hair is strongly influenced by food intake.

Two of the most common signs of severe fat restriction are hair loss and dry, scaly or infected skin. As well, high carbohydrate diets have repeatedly been associated with increased sebum production. What's wrong with having too much of this thick, waxy discharge? First of all, acne patients produce high levels of sebum. Secondly, excess scalp sebum leads to hair loss.

In addition, a 1976 study published in the *Southern Medical Journal* looked at over 1000 subjects and found that the intake of refined carbohydrates was significantly associated with skin abnormalities. Again, we know that sugar speed and total carbohydrate consumption is more useful than focussing on "refined carbohydrate."

Meanwhile, Minoxidol™ appears to be the only useful topical application for hair loss. This costly product works only in certain people, and once started, must be continued for a lifetime. Stopping its use will not only cause loss of new hair, but loss of much of the hair you started with.

Similarly, the new drug for balding, Propecia (finasteride), has been clinically proven to reduce hair loss in some men with male pattern baldness. The drug works by blocking levels of the hormone, dihydrotestosterone (DHT). However, unwanted side effects have been reported and is not recommended for women or children.

Our dietary guidelines help you restore your genetic potential for healthy skin and hair. Simply eating fatty fish a few times a week or taking low dose fish oil supplements is a good start. Careful attention to your protein and carbohydrate intake will improve the appearance of hair and skin. However, hair grows slowly, so give it time. As mentioned previously, natural progesterone is also useful in promoting hair growth for pre and menopausal women.

Sports Performance

Consider obesity and / or chronic illnesses as being at one end of a continuum, with exceptional athletic performance at the other end. Somewhere in the middle lies everyone else. Is there any evidence that athletic performance is enhanced by dietary interventions that control insulin levels? Dr. Barry Sears' work with elite athletes has shown that dietary control of insulin can result in superior athletic performance.

Hundreds of athletes, including professional football players, basketball stars, world class volleyball players, and Olympic swimmers have benefited from following a dietary program aimed at limiting insulin.

Los Angeles Raiders strength coach, Marv Marinovich worked with Dr. Sears to do a controlled study over a six week period. Dietary modifications resulted in remarkable performance benefits. Athletes significantly improved their agility, cardiovascular fitness, power and endurance.

These football players gained about 11 pounds, but lost 20% of their body fat over a six-week period. The men also gained an average of 16 pounds of lean body mass. And despite the muscle weight gain, they increased their vertical jump from about 33 inches to an average of 36 inches. Statistical analysis showed that if you repeated the experiment 10,000 times you would be likely to get the same results 9,995 times.

But perhaps the most remarkable benefits of Dr. Sear's dietary changes came for the members of the Stanford swim team. Pavlo Moralis, who had not swum for three years, came back and won two gold medals at the Barcelona Olympics. Similarly, Ginny Thompson broke the world record for the 100-meter freestyle. Angie Westercraig, at age 28, became the oldest woman to win the 100-meter and 200-meter butterfly in the National Championships. Likewise, 29-year-old Angel Martino became the oldest woman to make the Olympic swim team. She qualified in five different events. These athletes all followed dietary guidelines aimed at controlling insulin levels while optimizing micronutrient intake.

Limiting insulin secretion has been shown to increase the rate of oxygen transfer to the muscle cells, improve access to stored body fat and boost maximum aerobic performance. Elite athletes on an insulin limiting diet simply consume adequate amounts of protein and carbohydrate with higher levels of mono-unsaturated fat for calories.

Although many sports physiologists are still buying into the high carbohydrate myth, there is no scientific evidence to support the idea that *long-term* adherence to high carbohydrate diets improves athletic performance. New research has shown that a combination of protein and carbohydrate does a better job of replacing muscle glycogen than carbohydrates alone.

The bottom line is that most athletes have to try it before they believe it. Unfortunately, many won't even consider changing their diet because they refuse to believe in the potential for better results. It makes perfect sense that if our dietary modification works to improve all the cardiovascular measures in overweight heart patients, it should also act to benefit elite athletes.

Longevity

No one wants to live a long time without also enjoying good health. Quality of life is what this book is about, but our recommendations can also extend your life span.

The first step toward living a long life is avoidance of what might be referred to as the "deadly landmines." These landmines include such things as excessive smoking or drinking, abusing drugs, wearing black while night jogging, reckless driving and similar accident-prone activities.

Unfortunately, landmines also include questionable medical "help" such as surgery, prescription drugs or other interventions. Doctors can and do save lives, but consumer advocate Ralph Nader reports that medical interventions kill over 300,000 Americans every year. So think carefully before trusting any prescription drug, surgery or medical procedure. Get a second opinion. Also ask to speak to several living patients who have taken the same medication or undergone the same test, surgery or procedure.

The next step to a long life is to prevent the vast array of chronic or degenerative illnesses that typically bring on early death. Many of these were discussed in previous chapters. But we have yet to mention the clinical measures that tend to accompany both chronic diseases and the aging process. So let's look at some of the results of over 30 years of aging research.

Dr. Richard Weindruch, Ph.D. and associate professor of medicine at the University of California, has devoted most of his career to the study of food and longevity. One of his articles, published in a 1996 edition of *Scientific American*, examines caloric restriction and aging. Some of his key findings include:

- Eating less food, while consuming adequate protein, fat, vitamins and minerals, significantly increases life span in a variety of animals (no mention of carbohydrates).

- The dietary advice just listed tends to succeed, *even if it is started in middle age.*

- Restricting food intake clearly reduces the risk of developing cancer. This is related to low levels of circulating insulin.

- Although restricting food intake by up to 50% (compared to free feeding animals) increases life span the most, less severe restriction, even started in later life, also provides benefits.

- Calorie restricted animals not only live longer, but they appear to have a better quality of life. They are more active, have greater muscle mass and maintain their ability to learn.

- Supplementation alone with multivitamins or high dose antioxidants does not prolong life.

- Eating fewer calories while maintaining an appropriate nutrient intake involves regular use of nutrient dense foods or supplements.

- As monkeys and humans grow older, their blood pressure, blood glucose and blood insulin levels tend to rise. Aging also decreases insulin sensitivity or the ability of cells to remove insulin from the blood.

- One of the keys to limiting food intake is to control appetite (adequate protein and fat intake increase feelings of satisfaction).

Dr. Weindruch and his colleagues have been conducting two major trials of food restriction in monkeys. These have been in progress for over five years. The following chart compares many of the well-accepted measures of health between the two groups:

	Free Feeding Monkey	Food Restricted, Yet Adequate Nutrient Monkey
Food intake: *(kilocalories per day)*	688	477
Body weight: *(pounds)*	31	21
Percent body fat:	25%	10%
Accepted Health Measures:		
Blood Pressure *(systole/diastole)*	129/60	121/51
Glucose *(milligrams per deciliter of blood)*	71	56
Insulin level *(microunits per milliliter of blood)*	93	29
Triglycerides *(milligrams per deciliter of blood)*	169	67

It is clear that many of the biological measures that typically rise with age are changing more slowly in food restricted monkeys. Although blood pressure at this snapshot was only slightly lower in the restricted food group, the research authors note that it had been markedly lower for much of the five-year study period.

One of the main problems with helping humans to restrict calories is appetite, both biochemical and psychological. Most health professionals are aware of the benefits of limiting food intake, yet many find it difficult to successfully curb even their own appetites.

The secret lies in using adequate amounts of high quality protein. In the words of University of Toronto nutrition professor, Dr. David Jenkins, "protein acts to put the brakes on appetite." Dr. Jenkins work also shows that excess flour consumption causes persistent hyperglycemia that typically results in chronic hunger. In addition, when we know how much protein and fat our bodies require, we can spread this intake throughout the day in a way that will prevent overeating.

The second key to curbing appetite is to ingest sufficient amounts of vitamins, minerals and trace minerals. If our bodies are well nourished, we suppress the desire to eat more food. An activity called pica and cribbing (the tendency to eat non-food) typically results from micronutrient deficiencies. Children who eat dried paint, dirt, window sealant and other non-food substances are usually malnourished. Furthermore, pregnant women with food cravings are often deficient in micronutrients because the fetus is using nutrients that are not being sufficiently replaced.

Farmers have been giving animals vitamin and mineral supplements for decades in a successful bid to promote the health of livestock and prevent damage to farmland and equipment. Veterinarian, physician and author, Dr. Joel Wallach, emphasizes the importance of vitamin and mineral intake to human health.

Food advertisers try to convince us that pica and cribbing is not a deficiency of nutrients. They like to call it "the munchies." And when the munchies hit, their promotions tell us to reach for junk food. Pretzels, chips, candy, cookies, crackers, curly fries and thousands of similiar foods are loaded with empty calories. These products make us crave more because they don't solve the underlying problem of poor nutrition.

So restricting food intake to nutrient rich calories acts to limit appetite and control insulin. And if animal studies aren't enough to convince you about the role of insulin in longevity, then consider the people of a small village in a region of Russia known as Abkhasia. People here commonly live past the age of 100 and there have been unconfirmed reports of some living to the age of 140.

Their restrictive diet is composed of vitamin rich vegetables and meat with small amounts of dairy products, nuts and fruit. Their food is grown in mineral rich soil. In addition, Abkasians are known to regularly walk up to 20 miles a day and daily physical labor is ingrained in their culture. Records show that people over the age of 90 continue to be paid for full time work in the tea fields.

While you may not be willing to work in the tea fields or walk 20 miles a day, you can still alter your food intake and activity to gain significant benefits. The important message is that most

Abkasians will certainly have *low levels of insulin,* while consuming adequate nutrients.

Insulin, not dietary fat, is the villain that leads to a shortened life span. A 1992 study published in the International *Journal of Aging and Human Development* found that adults who lived past the age of 100 were less likely to consume diets low in fat, when compared to those who died at an earlier age.

Restricting food intake is not the only method that has been proven to increase the life span of animals. Adding EPA (primarily from fish fat) can significantly lengthen life span. It has also been linked to the prevention of cancer. In addition, EPA is a powerful inhibitor of the enzyme that makes arachidonic acid. This acid causes a variety of health problems.

8.

Super Simple Steps

The Food Game

Goals are easy to achieve when they are broken down into small steps. Simply begin, and read this chapter more than once. One exposure to new

The game: on target for results.

139

information rarely imprints the message or makes it part of our ongoing knowledge. Education is repetition and education is repetition.

No two people are the same. We each have different taste preferences, food beliefs, physical requirements and genetic traits. Individual experimentation and flexibility are desirable. There is, however, an optimal range of macronutrient intake based on a scientifically measurable hormone response that applies to the majority of human beings. The food game method is a powerful, yet easy *starting point* toward better health.

The amount of food listed in the following columns (pp. 142-146) is for a lightly active, 150 pound adult, of average height and build. If you have a large frame, are muscular or physically active, you will need more calories. Limit your carbohydrate intake. Do not be afraid to add more protein or fat. The more active you are, the more good fat you will need to consume.

Remember to eat at least three meals a day and add small snacks, as needed, to *prevent excess hunger.* Do not go more than 5 hours without eating a balanced meal or snack. Always eat breakfast within one hour of getting up.

You can make food taste great by using spices, no-cal brand syrups, flavor extracts, mustard, salt, pepper and garlic. You can also use zero or low carbohydrate salad dressing, sugar free gelatins and small amounts of sugar free puddings. Read labels and look for zero or low carbohydrate content.

It is *extremely* important to add fat. Fat is your friend in health and weight loss because it slows the absorption of sugars into the bloodstream. It also makes you feel satisfied.

Beginner Level:
Starting Point to Better Health

Play the 4 Choice Food Game:

1) Create any meal by choosing one food item from each of the four columns. Drink a glass of water before and with meals.

2) Create any snack by choosing one-third of the amount of any food item from each column. Drink water before snacks.

3) See further on for more tips and to adjust the **amount** of food needed to suit your unique size and activity level.

Play the Four Choice Food Game (see previous page for instructions)

A. Protein		B. Carb #1		C. Carb #2		D. Fats	
Approx. 20 grams of protein		Approx. 10 grams of carbohydrate		Approx. 15 grams of carbohydrate		Less than **5** grams of fat	
** best choices		All good		** best choices		** best choices	
Note: 4 oz = 1/4 pound or 120 grm. Of weight		Bamboo shoots	11/2 c	Apple sauce	1/2c	Olive oil **	1 tsp
Salmon**	4 oz	Beans (green)	1 c	Banana (small)	1/2	Avocado ** or guacamole	3 tbs
Mackerel**	4 oz	Beans (yellow)	1 c	Blackberries	3/4c	Canola oil	1 tsp
Sardines**	3 oz	Broccoli	11/4 c	Blueberries	3/4c	Peanut oil	1 tsp
Tuna***	4 oz	Brussel Sprouts	11/4 c	Cantaloupe** (small)	1/2	Peanut Btr.	2 tsp
Sole	4 oz	Cabbage	2 c	Cherries**	3/4c	Almonds**	9
Haddock	4 oz	Cauliflower (cut)	11/2 c	Cranberries** (raw)	1/4c	Slivered nuts	3 tsp

Halibut	4 oz	Celery	11/2 c	Cranberry sauce	3tsp	Almond Btr.	1 tsp
Herring	4 oz	Cucumber	11/2 c	Dates	2	Cashews**	9
Whitefish	4 oz	Eggplant	11/4 c	Figs	1	Brazil nuts	2
Trout	4 oz	Fiddlehead	3 c	Fruit cocktail	1/2c	Pistachios	12
Seafood:		Lettuce	5 c	Grapefruit** (large)	1/2	Macadamia**	3
Clams	4 oz	Mushrooms	3 c	Grapes**	1/2c	Tahini	2 tsp
Crab	4 oz	Onions (raw)	3/4 c	Kiwi (large)	1	**Poor Choices**	
Lobster	4 oz	Parsnips	1/4 c	Mangos	1/2	Mayonnaise (light)	3 tsp
Oysters	4 oz	Peppers	11/4 c	Nectarine	1	Butter	1 tsp
Scallops	4 oz	Radishes	21/2c	Orange** (small)	1	Cream	1 tbs
Shrimp	4 oz	Spinach	6 c	Papayas	1/2	Sour cream	1 tbs
Soy "Meats"		Tomato (raw)	11/4 c	Peaches**	1	Low fat	3 tbs
Firm tofu**	6 oz	Turnips	1 c	Pears (small)	1	Margarine	1 tsp
Soy slices**	3			Pineapple (diced)	3/4c	Lard	1 tsp

continues ...

... continued

Food	Amount		Food	Amount		Food	Amount
Soy hotdogs**	2		**Starchy Veges:**			Plums (small)	2
Soy burger	11/2		Poor choices:			Prunes	2
Soy bacon	4					Raspberries**	1 c
Protein powder** (read label)	1 tbsp		c = cup			Rhubarb (raw)	2 c
			Baked beans	1/8 c		Strawberries	1 c
Poultry / Meat:			Kidney beans	1/4 c		Tangerines	1
Chicken breast**	3oz		Beets	1/2 c		Watermelon slice	1/2
Turkey breast**	3 oz		Carrots	1/2 c			
Ostrich**	3 oz		Potatoes	1/3 c		Pasta / Rice etc.	
Rabbit	3 oz		(mashed)	1/5 c		(poor choices)	
Lean lamb	3 oz		Corn	1/4 c		(amount after cooking)	
Veal	3 oz		Lima beans	1/4 c			

Item	Amount	Item	Amount	Item	Amount
Lean ham	3 oz	Squash	1/2 c	Egg noodles	1/3c
Lean pork	3 oz	Lentils	1/4 c	Noodles (chow mein)	1/2c
Poultry (drk)	3 oz	Parsnip	1/3 c	Spaghetti	1/3c
Duck	4 oz	Chick peas	1/4 c	Macaroni	1/3c
Back bacon	3 oz	Soybeans	1/2 c	Rice (brown)	1/3c
Lean hot dogs	2	Peas	1/3 c	Rice (white)	1/3c
Lean beef	3 oz	Rutabagas	1 c	Rice cake (med)	1
Eggs / Dairy c = cup		**Breads etc:**		**Sweets**	
Egg whites**	6	Saltines	4	Caramels	2
Whole eggs	3	Wheat Thins	6	Gum drops	4
Egg subst.**	3/4 c	Croutons	12	Jelly beans	5
1% cottage	3/4 c	Bagels	1/4 c	Licorice	2
Cheese	3/4 c	Melba Toast	4	Marshmallow	3
Skim ricotta	6 oz	Pita pocket	1/4	Baker's choc square	1
Skim Mozzarella	3 oz	Bread slice	1/2		
		Rye slice	1/2		

continues …

... continued

Food	Amount	Food	Amount	Food	Amount
Low fat Cheese	3 oz	English muffin	1/4 c	"Caramilk" bar	3/4
String Cheese	3 oz	Taco shell	1	"Oh Henry" bar	1
		white bread	1 slc	Cream cookie	2
Combination Dairy				Arrowroot cookie	3
(= 20 grams protein and 28 grams carbo – limit)		**Cereals / grains etc:**		Fig bar	1
1% milk	3 c	All Bran	1tbs	Sweetened coconut	1/4 c
Plain yogurt	1 1/2c	Barley (dry)	1/2 c	Cupcake (small)	1
Milk powder (instant)	2 1/4c	Bran flakes	1/4 c	Icecream	1/2c
		Granola	1/4 c		
		Oatmeal** (cooked)	1/3 c	**Alcohol:**	
		Rice crispies	1/2 c	One beer or 50 ml spirits or	Lite
		Shredd wheat	1/4 c	1-2 glasses of dry wine.	Per day
		Popcorn	1 1/2 c		

- End -

Suit Yourself Adjustments:

Although we recommend that you eat at least three meals plus a mid afternoon and evening snack, you may wish to follow a different routine. Active people usually like to include a mid morning snack. One of my patients eats a very small amount of the correct food mix every two hours. Although most people find this too inconvenient, it works for her. She has lost excess body fat and is enjoying excellent health.

Experiment to find the meal and snack pattern that suits your needs. Keep in mind that the human body functions best when given small amounts of food on a regular basis. Choose an anxiety free and hunger free system that you can live with for the rest of your life. *Write it down.* Writing engages the sub-conscious mind and leads to appropriate action.

Write it down. Engage your subconscious.

Follow your chosen eating times as often as possible. The human body likes routine. There will be times, however, when you can't follow your normal eating pattern, so adjust snacks accordingly. The key is to *prevent hunger* and overeating. If you wait until you feel hungry before eating then you are more likely to overeat. Hunger is a sign of low blood sugar and it takes your brain about 30 minutes *after you begin eating* to register feelings of satisfaction. A lot of food can be downed over a 30-minute time span.

Remember that food is like a drug. For any drug delivery system, the mix, timing and amount taken is critical for achieving the desired results. Several studies have shown that eating the right mix of small amounts of food will improve blood glucose, insulin and cholesterol levels.

The health outcome you achieve from the foods you eat can be compared to the results a doctor might see from the *right mix and timing* of intravenous drugs. What are you "dripping" into your bloodstream every day via the foods you eat?

Regularly eating the right mix of food helps to control weight. For example, a 1996 study published in the *European Journal of Clinical Nutrition* states that "individuals who snack throughout the day have positive advantages in terms of body weight control."

In addition, an October 1996 study published in *The Scandinavian Journal of Medicine & Science* compared people who ate six meals a day with people who ate two meals a day (same amount and type of food). The authors found that "The lower frequency of meal intake leads to greater muscle loss, even if exactly the same diet is consumed." In other words, one loses more lean muscle when eating two meals per day than when eating exactly the same food spread out over six small meals. Muscle is something we want to keep.

Your body becomes very good at storing fat when you skip meals and essentially put it on famine alert.

Small, but frequent food intake acts to turn up body temperature and resting metabolic rate. The higher your metabolic rate, the more calories you burn, even while sleeping.

Playing the food game will help you to consume an appropriate mix of macronutrients. If you feel hungry and want more food, then avoid the carbohydrates and simply add more from the protein or fat columns. Eat until you feel comfortably satisfied. Drinking water also helps diminish hunger.

Although bread and pasta are listed as choices in the food column list, those with serious weight or health problems would be best to avoid these. As mentioned earlier, Ph.D. pharmacologist, Dr. Robert Gaskin, believes that wheat based products are at the root of chronic ill health.

You can estimate food intake by:

1) Easiest way: Look at the palm of your hand. At each meal, consume about a palm sized portion of protein (and no thicker than your palm). For snacks, choose about a thumb size portion of protein. You can always eat less protein, as long as this amount satisfies your appetite and prevents overeating.

When you choose carbohydrates from the preferred items on the list (starred), then eat about twice the volume of carbohydrate as your protein choice. For example, a double palm sized portion of mixed fibrous vegetables. If you are choosing high sugar speed carbohydrates, such as bread or potatoes, then eat only the same volume of carbohydrates as the volume of your protein choice. You may, however, find it best to avoid this type of carbohydrate. And remember to *always add a small amount of fat* (see food column list for type and amount).

or

2) How do you compare against this "average" woman with the following qualities?

Height:	5 ft 7 inches
Weight:	150 pounds
% body fat:	30%
Activity level:	lightly active (1.5 hrs/wk)
Daily Protein intake:	about 75 grams/day

This 75 grams would be divided and spread out over a number of meals and snacks.

Most men and many women will be larger in size and have more lean muscle mass. Some will also engage in high levels of physical exercise. Compare yourself with this "average" woman described above. Based on your size and activity level, do you think you should be eating more or less protein? Experiment to see how much protein and fat will satisfy your hunger and match this with an appropriate amount of carbohydrate.

If you regularly do heavy exercise, then you will need a bit more protein (start with an extra 7 grams daily) and more mono-unsaturated fat, than an inactive person. Never eat more than 35 grams of protein at any one sitting. What does 35 grams look like? For most protein rich foods, it would be about the palm size and thickness of a very large man's hand. It would also be about four level tablespoons of most protein powders (but read the label).

Advanced Level

Another way to play the food game is to ask yourself which one of the following three categories you *best* fit into:

A. You have Type I or Type II diabetes. You may be thin or overweight.

B. You have too much body fat and find it difficult to lose weight or to stop gaining weight **or** you suffer from some form of chronic illness or pain.

C. You are slim or underweight. You find it difficult to gain weight or to build muscle mass. You may or may not have some abnormal medical test results.

Which of the previous three categories applies to you?

A — read category A information

B — read category B information

C — read category C information

Category A:

You have Type I or Type II diabetes. You may be thin or overweight.

This section will describe some key points about diabetes and nutrition. Although a detailed description of diabetes is beyond our scope, we encourage anyone with an interest in this common condition to read the book *Dr. Bernstein's Diabetes Solution.*

Dr. Richard Bernstein writes from the unique perspective of someone who has lived with Type I diabetes for over 50 years. The author's unconventional methods have successfully prevented and even reversed many of the potentially devastating complications of diabetes. He emphasizes the importance of restricting carbohydrate intake. His book is a remarkable and potentially life saving resource for people with both Type I or Type II diabetes.

Key Points about Diabetes:

The number one priority in diabetes is to control blood glucose (sugar) levels. There is conclusive evidence to show that normalizing blood glucose will dramatically reduce the likelihood of blindness, kidney failure, nerve damage, amputations and even heart attacks.

The importance of prevention cannot be overemphasized. My biggest frustration over the past ten years of hospital work has been to see the needless suffering of so many diabetes patients. Many have gone blind, had amputations, strokes or other complications.

Such people will often say "I'll do anything to get better, I'll follow any diet, I'll do exactly as you say." Unfortunately, prevention is better than treatment. Dietary changes that help normalize blood glucose levels can prevent and even reverse serious complications.

If you have diabetes, today is the time to act. The only way to prevent complications is to control blood glucose levels. Any dietitian will tell you that the single greatest factor affecting post-meal blood glucose is the amount of carbohydrate consumed. Even the American Diabetes Association recently issued new food guidelines emphasizing this point.

Most people know why carbohydrate restriction works for Type II or obesity related diabetes, yet few people understand how this applies to the Type I condition. Type I diabetes usually occurs before the age of 40 and results in the loss of ability to make insulin. Survival depends on the use of insulin injections.

When carbohydrate input is limited, it also decreases the amount of injected insulin needed to control blood sugar. This then reduces the entire variability of the system. Large additions to any system that requires balance, tend to cause instability. Dr. Bernstein refers to this idea as the "law of small numbers." It is an accepted aspect of systems control theory in engineering. Hey, it also makes perfect sense.

So what should you be eating if you have diabetes? Like Dr. Bernstein and thousands of his satisfied patients (many of whom are physicians), eat a low carbohydrate diet. After all, diabetes is also known as glucose intolerance. It is not called protein intolerance or fat intolerance. Ironically, conventional dietary advice tells people with diabetes to eat more of the very foods that they can't tolerate!

Eating a low carbohydrate diet means choosing your foods mainly from the protein or fat columns, along with reasonable amounts of low glycemic carbohydrates such as fibrous vegetables. You can also use several low or no carbohydrate foods listed later in this book.

You may be able to add small amounts of fruit and a little starchy vegetable. Add only to the point of still being able to control blood glucose. Your test for average blood glucose (physicians call it the "HbA1C test") should also stay within the normal range. This test is an excellent predictor of your likelihood for developing future complications. Ask your doctor for a written copy of the normal range of results for this test.

People with diabetes need to limit carbohydrate. Now you might say "but then I have to eat more protein or more fat and doesn't protein damage your kidneys? Doesn't fat clog your blood vessels?" There is no truth to the belief that adequate protein causes kidney damage. Dr. Bernstein and others have shown this to be one of the biggest myths of modern medicine.

Even Professor of Renal Medicine, Dr. N.P. Mallick debunked this still common belief in a 1994 article published in the October issue of the *British Medical Journal*. There is also no evidence to suggest that eating fat, while restricting carbohydrates, clogs blood vessels.

Whether you have diabetes or any other illness, you are wise to arm yourself with plenty of information. Ask yourself where the information is coming from and what the potential interests are of those providing it. Moreover, do what works for you. This doesn't mean just assessing how you feel, but also knowing about standard medical tests that measure risk factors for future complications.

Category B:

You have too much body fat and find it difficult to lose weight or to stop gaining weight *or* you suffer from some form of chronic illness or pain.

Dietary amounts listed in the food column list will be a good starting point for you. If you still feel hungry, then simply add more fat and protein. Continue to limit carbohydrates. Remember that there is no danger in getting most of your calories from protein, fat, fibrous vegetables and small amounts of fruit.

Adjust your food intake by asking yourself how you feel about two or three hours after a meal. If you feel very hungry and foggy-headed then you probably ate too much carbohydrate. Drinking water or chewing sugar free gum can also help, but don't be afraid to have a little protein-rich snack. Eat small amounts frequently during the day to avoid overeating in the evenings.

Category C:

You are slim or underweight. You find it difficult to gain weight or to build muscle mass by exercising. You may be interested in sports performance.

Are you the type of person who can eat almost anything and not gain weight? While many will envy your genetics, you are still susceptible to poor health. Those who are thin can experience fatigue, high blood pressure, high triglyceride levels, excess blood insulin and other problems.

Thin people may have a family history of heart disease or other illnesses. Even if you are generally healthy with only an occasional headache or premenstrual discomfort you will find our dietary guidelines to be useful. They will boost your energy levels and extend your life.

If one of your goals is to gain weight then the only healthy approach is to gain more muscle, not more body fat. Unfortunately, no quantity of food or supplement alone will build muscle without exercise. Weight training is the best muscle strengthening exercise and women benefit just as much as men. They needn't fear looking excessively muscular or losing their femininity. It won't happen unless you devote a lot of time and effort toward becoming a serious body builder.

Weight training causes the release of growth hormone, which is one of the most powerful youth generating substances known. Growth hormone injections can also increase fat loss, build lean muscle mass and skin thickness. But unlike exercise, these injections are controversial. Some scientists believe that injections do nothing to increase muscle strength, maximum oxygen consumption or improved cognitive function. The bottom line is that weight training exercise is the safest way to benefit.

Repetition with light weights will build strength without excess bulk. Some basic rules for lifting include keeping your back straight, lifting a weight 8–10 times (one set) for three repetitions and resting for no longer than one minute between sets. You don't need any fancy equipment and simple wall push offs or knee push-ups are a good way to start. You can also use inexpensive hand weights or rubber expansion bands. Weight training needs to be a regular habit but the same exercises should be done *no more* than every second day.

Building muscle requires protein, but the average recreational weight lifter needs no more than seven additional grams of protein per day. Further caloric requirements should be added in the form of mono-unsaturated fat. Athletes who over consume carbohydrates often struggle in their attempts to build muscle mass. This occurs because high insulin levels *decrease the production of growth hormone.*

9.

Life Leaves Clues

We have only to move in the direction of our dreams to meet with a success unknown in common hours.

Henry David Thoreau

Taking Charge

Media personality Oprah Winfrey once said that the question she is most frequently asked is, "how do you stay motivated?" Her typical response emphasizes the importance of a positive mental attitude and an absolute faith in specific and favorable outcomes. Unfortunately, this knowledge alone rarely leads to appropriate action.

So why do some people achieve and maintain their health and lifestyle goals while others fail? What makes successful people different from those who report low levels of satisfaction? Are successful people just luckier than others? Are they born better looking and smarter, with better brains and better genes? Do all successful people come from the best schools and have nurturing, wealthy parents? Do they travel one easy road leading from achievement to achievement? The answers are no, no, no and no.

Extensive research looking at thousands of subjects has shown that physical attractiveness, though emphasized in our culture, has virtually nothing to do with happiness. Intelligence, age and education also show no direct correlation with reports of well-being. So who gains continuing fulfillment and satisfaction?

Long-term satisfaction occurs when *we become aware of our ability to make good things happen in our lives and when we see ourselves as the cause of these events.* This explains why lottery winners rarely report increased levels of long term happiness. While a certain minimum income contributes to well-being, additional money rarely brings greater health or satisfaction.

Success in most areas, including health, has to do with a realization that we have the power to control and change our behavior. Acknowledging and accepting that we alone are responsible for our outcomes is vital to well-being. And it is never too late to change the doubts we hold about our abilities. We can stop depending on others, or worse still, blaming others. Blaming never improves the situation.

So the only consistently proven difference between healthy, successful people and unsuccessful people is that they *think* in certain ways. Their thinking habits cause them to take appropriate action. Enough thoughtful and reasonable action leads to the desired results. And the sum of all our actions determines the quality of our lives.

Are your current thoughts and beliefs helping you to reach the outcomes you desire? Are you aware of what you are thinking? Are you open to new possibilities? What do you really want to be doing with your life? Do you know about the thousands of options? As Sir Anthony Hopkins once said "what one person can do, another can learn to do." This does not mean we can all be brain surgeons, but choices are plentiful.

The way we think also influences how persistent we will be when faced with criticism or other difficulties. Many people simply give up when faced with challenges. We've all heard those who say things like "I'm never doing this again" or "it's all too hard." Another popular response to criticism is to get mad at the person giving you negative feedback.

What if we simply thanked others for their valuable, though critical input? Choosing not to feel hurt is a decision. We can learn more from the blunt criticism of strangers, than from friends who don't want to hurt our feelings. This doesn't mean we have to agree with everyone, but hearing and thinking about various opinions is useful. Carefully listening to criticism and adjusting our actions accordingly leads to better results.

Successful people also know when to separate who they are from what happens to them. For example, the tragedy of suicide can result when someone is unable to detach themselves from painful emotions. Yet we can rise above any sorrow. We are more solid than the thoughts we experience.

Successful people also see failure as opportunity. They welcome problems and persistently search for solutions. They know that any difficulty can be either solved or managed. They think "I can solve this when, or I can solve this after, or I can solve this with, or I can solve this little by little." Their thoughts and actions lead to positive results.

Unfortunately, too many people fail to take appropriate action until it is too late. If we fail to act on life, life will make things happen that we won't enjoy. In fact, most North Americans have an unhealthy addiction to safety, security and inertia. And this safe inaction goes hand in hand with depression.

While depression is a complex illness, psychiatrists know that sufferers typically perceive and think about their world differently from those who enjoy good mental health. For example, one person entering a restaurant may see a lively atmosphere, pleasant aromas and beautiful decorations, while another only notices the spotty forks, hard chairs and loud noises. One person finds joyful opportunities while another feels dissatisfied.

Dr. Norman Vincent Peale first popularized the importance of how we think or our cognitive behavior, in his book *The Power of Positive Thinking*. While several critics bemoaned this approach as overly simplistic, behavioral scientists have since verified many of his ideas.

Positive thinking, however, does not mean that we must always think "good thoughts." When negative thoughts appear, and they will, we can acknowledge and observe them but not *dwell* on them. Look at the negativity but avoid the paralysis of over-analysis.

In addition, there is an important factor that must co-exist with positive thinking, but it is often overlooked. *Positive thinking cannot work if we continue to hold a negative self-image.* As author Dr. Maxwell Maltz writes, "it is literally impossible to think positively about a particular situation as long as you hold a negative concept of self." Positive thinking creates valuable results only after people realize their unique worth, power and potential.

This is why basic techniques like daily reminders of what we have accomplished (even simple things) and what we have to be thankful for, can work wonders. Write a list of several things you have done

Troubled by low self-worth, Ann takes a job as a speed bump.

in life that took effort to achieve. Review your list regularly. Listen also to the words that you say to yourself. Are you your own best cheerleader, or are you critical? Simple habits create the desired results.

Positive thinking also has nothing to do with simply smiling and pretending everything is wonderful. It is a method for honestly facing problems, looking for solutions and *taking action*. Positive thinkers learn to see multiple solutions for life's inevitable challenges.

Power of Conditioning

So why do some people think positively and believe in themselves, while others feel like helpless victims? Although genetics and physiology play a role, our environment is undoubtedly a big factor. Our subconscious mind is programmed from the moment of birth. Any reasonable psychologist can verify the power of subconscious conditioning and its role in determining behavior.

Unfortunately, as the word implies, most of us are unaware of the forceful messages and *belief systems* held within our subconscious. Just as a computer is provided with various inputs, so too is the human brain. With enough time and persistence, we can change our beliefs as easily as we change a computer disk. Altering your subconscious conditioning can literally save your life.

In a prosperous and democratic society, what we believe to be true about our world and ourselves determines the nature of our lives. The maps we hold of reality create our experiences. Unfortunately, even highly intelligent and educated people can be stuck with mental maps that limit their success. Where did these maps come from? They were created by parents, teachers, friends, television, radio, advertisements and dozens of other influences.

The good news is that time and re-programming can successfully improve our outcomes. A willingness to deeply examine our beliefs and their source of origin is the first step toward success. So what does all this have to do with food and health?

Food and Thoughts

Much has been written about the relationship between destructive eating patterns and how we think. Negative family habits, emotional upset, boredom, low self-esteem, lack of love, past abuse and other psychological obstacles all influence food habits. What we accept to be true about ourselves has an influence over our day to day health habits.

Anne Fletcher emphasizes this idea in her book *Thin for Life*. She interviewed 160 people who had successfully lost at least 20 pounds and were able to keep it off for three or more years. She found that the most common factor shared by these people was a realization that they alone had the power to improve their health and their lives. They stopped blaming other people and began making small changes to their daily routines.

They also began to visualize what they wanted in the *long term*. There is truth in the saying "where

there is no vision, the people perish." Believing in our ability to shape the future gives us a sense of individual control. As one of my diabetes patients said "my life changed when I began to believe in me."

So one of the first steps to better health and motivation is to examine our thoughts. Many people with health problems say things like "I've tried everything to lose weight" or "nothing will control my blood sugar" or "I just can't eat breakfast," or "I must have my morning coffee." None of these statements are true, but they become self-fulfilling. We make it so by saying it is so.

History has proven that there are universal ways of thinking that create success, but this doesn't mean we have to be overly smart. Even brilliant intellectualism will fail without *subconscious* self-acceptance. We've all known intelligent men and women who lead mediocre lives and are out of touch with their spirit. They are unable to love themselves or others because they cannot give what they do not have. They also live in denial. Fortunately, it is never too late to reprogram our thoughts and make peace with who we are.

Two Keys to Healthy Eating

Healthy eating involves two factors:

 1. The correct macronutrient mix that will satisfy your physical needs, prevent cravings

and balance brain chemistry (chapters one to eight in this book) and

 2. How to influence the *subconscious* mind and create a *way of thinking* that will enable you to continue healthy habits for the rest of your life (this chapter).

Nutritional success comes from knowing what to do and how to keep doing it. Food then becomes merely an enjoyable way of maintaining good health. Fatigue or illness won't distract you from pursuing your goals and interests. You will start to think less about food and more about abundant living. Health enables us to create purpose and meaning in our lives. And freedom to act in pursuit of our dreams is the height of what life has to offer.

Reprogramming

There are *specific tech-niques* that can be used to dramatically alter our thoughts and actions. These have been scientifically verified by several people including Pro-fessor David McClelland at the  Harvard University Achievement and Motivation Project and Professor Warren Bennice at the University of Southern California School of Business.

These techniques have also been used by hundreds of famous people including W. Clement

Stone, Lee Iaccoca, Fran Tarkington, Mary Lou Rhetton, Jack Nicholas, Arnold Swarzenegger, Mohammed Ali, Bruce Jenner, Jack Canfield and many others. These methods are practical and they produce results.

Never too late

Not all successful people have had to consciously learn and practice specific techniques to alter their thinking. Some are brought up in environments that encourage social, physical and emotional well-being. Children may be told *thousands of times, over many years* how valuable, intelligent and capable they are. Some are exposed to ever increasing challenges and they learn to succeed. Such kids internalize positive subconscious messages about themselves, their world and their potential. They develop what psychologists call core self-esteem.

Unfortunately, few people have had an ideal childhood. Families can create fear and distrust. For example, alcoholic parents who cannot look after themselves are unlikely to give appropriate care to a growing child. Children who receive inadequate attention feel unworthy and helpless. They may even feel responsible for making their parents happy.

Similar dysfunction occurs when relatives do not listen to each other. Family members become mentally sick when they cannot speak openly about important issues or when there is little attempt at understanding. Painfully obvious facts may be ignored, as if they didn't exist.

This is not meant to blame anyone. Parents or other caregivers typically do the best they can, given their level of knowledge, understanding and upbringing. They also carry burdens from their own childhood. Imagine your parents as five-year-old children and you will begin to see their vulnerability. Understanding can then replace any blame, frustration and anger, all of which serve no purpose.

Many adult characteristics and belief systems result from dysfunctional conditioning. The majority of my patients initially display thought patterns that damage their health, yet it is never too late to change. We can stop thinking, behaving and acting in ways that are destructive.

B.F. Skinner, the father of behavioral psychology, said, "humans are controlled by their environment." He wrote and spoke about the stimulus—response event. In other words, how we are trained to respond, often subconsciously, leads to certain outcomes.

Skinner, however, failed to mention that we can also *control and shape our environment*. We can choose what we will read or listen to on TV or movie screens, who to befriend, who to learn from, and much more. If we know how to change our sensory input or environment, then we start to think and react in ways that promote health and abundant living.

For example, author Jack Canfield uses the following equation:

$$E + R = O$$

Or **E**vent plus **R**esponse equals **O**utcome

If we don't like what is happening in our lives then we need to change our response. For example, if we're not healthy or we don't have enough money or our relationships aren't working, then the only solution is to choose a new response. If we keep believing and doing the same things, then we'll keep getting the same outcomes.

Unfortunately, the easiest or most natural response often creates the least favorable outcome. For example, it is easy to feel hurt and angry when someone attacks you, yet this action seldom improves the situation. Forgiveness, though difficult, is ultimately in our own best interests. Holding on to anger is inevitably self-destructive.

We can train ourselves to respond in ways that may not seem natural. Doing so requires accepting some initial discomfort. We learn to feel comfortable being uncomfortable. Frequent practice makes the task easier. Persistently trying enough responses creates the desired result. Unfortunately, many people give up too soon, but things often improve just as we're ready to admit defeat. The key is to hang on over the rough spots.

Is there an Ideal Environment?

If a child had a perfect upbringing, what would it look like? What are some of the characteristics of an ideal childhood or even adult environment?

It would include such things as:

- being well nourished and housed
- reasonable safety and security
- exposure to happy adult role models
- emotional support of family and friends
- being carefully listened to and learning to listen
- regular physical activity
- varied sensory input
- exposure to art, music and nature
- opportunities for challenge and risk taking
- freedom to make and learn from mistakes
- encouragement to express humor
- opportunities to be playful
- appropriate rewards for success
- freedom to talk about feelings and emotions
- acceptance and understanding of emotions
- involvement in group collaboration
- acceptance of human faults and frailties
- curiosity and joy of learning
- opportunities for spiritual growth
- appreciation of community involvement ... and more

What subconscious beliefs would develop in those who were raised in such an environment?

- The world can be a reasonably safe place.
- I am a valued person.
- I have the power to improve my life and the lives of others.
- It's okay to take risks and make mistakes.
- I know and accept my strengths and imperfections.
- I can forgive myself and others.
- I can love others and I am lovable.
- I can overcome or manage problems.
- I am optimistic and aware of possibilities.
- I am creative and have much to contribute.
- I can overcome fear.
- I can learn to do what others have done.
- If I ask enough people, I will gain help .
- I alone am responsible for my outcomes.
- I am able to change my thoughts and actions.
- I can experience joy, beauty and abundance.
- The rewards in life are worth the struggle.
- Difficult times can be managed and will pass.
- Focus and persistence are valuable traits.

Such ways of thinking and believing increase the likelihood that a child will grow into a successful and happy adult. So the question is—if we didn't get this sort of conditioning as children, then *why can't we start giving ourselves this environment, beginning right now?* We can create the appropriate conditioning input for ourselves, if we know how to do it.

It is also important to think long term. How many years did it take you to adopt your current way of thinking? If your present beliefs are providing you with the life you want, then there is no need to change. But if your life is falling short of your desires, then think long term.

Repetition is the key to all learning. Children in ideal environments have been told thousands of times that they can succeed. Adults need similar levels of repetition over long periods of time. Unfortunately, few people give this a chance, because their current thoughts hold them back. But the way to be like everyone else is to think like everyone else. Only a small percentage of people break away from the norm. As the philosopher, Voltaire said, "Every man is the creature of the age in which he lives; very few raise themselves above the ideas of the time."

Be willing to feel a bit silly and uncomfortable. This is a necessary part of the process. With enough time and persistence, you can change your conditioning and create the results you desire. Remember Winston Churchill's shortest speech ever, "When should we give up? Never, Never, Never."

This is not to say you can't pull the plug on something that is failing. But when failure occurs, and it will, acknowledge the setback and move on to the next goal.

You may wish to begin your new lifestyle by writing down and affirming to yourself, "I am happily improving my thoughts and actions. I am joyfully creating the success I desire." Or be very specific, for example, "I am happily finishing my project (whatever is important to you)."

Remember to use the words "I am" because the subconscious does not recognize future tense such as "I am going to do, or I will try to do or I would like to do, etc." It is also important to have a feeling word in your statement such as "I am happily, joyfully, gleefully, etc." because *it is how you think you will feel* that consistently motivates you to take appropriate action.

Affirmations can be uncomfortable because you might see them as lies, but the discomfort indicates an important need. If you say "I am healthy, strong and energetic," but in truth, you are fat, weak and lazy, then repeated affirmations move you toward change. They tell your subconscious that you are serious about this idea and it begins to work on finding solutions. You will start moving more, reading health books, eating wisely, noticing products that can help, exercising, and more. You will begin to *act* in ways that move your affirmations toward reality. There is nothing magical or mystical about it. It works because you start to take appropriate actions, but the discipline is in *continuing the affirmations.*

In the movie *The Edge* two men are being stalked by a grizzly bear and the only way they can survive is to kill the bear. The wise character played by Sir Anthony Hopkins says to his companion "I'm going to kill the bear ... say it again, say it louder ... I'm going to kill the bear!" Anyone who understands the subconscious mind will grasp the significance of this scene. They know that repetitive verbal expression of *intent* has great power to create the desired result. Note, however, that the more effective expression would be "I am killing the bear."

All this being said, you can affirm, set goals and visualize until the cows come home, but it is only persistent *action* that will create success. If you visualize and affirm enough, the motivation to act will appear. In fact, you will start to feel uncomfortable when you don't take enough action. Take small steps every day toward your goals. Move ahead and don't let your fears hold you back.

Unfortunately, we must often begin to take action without actually knowing how to proceed. As you act, your experience will give you feedback as to whether you are on the right track or not. Some people call this the "ready, fire, aim" method. Any success typically results from being off target most of the time. But each mistake shows us how to get closer to where we want to be. Fire, listen to feedback, readjust, aim again, fire, readjust, aim again and so on. Be willing to blunder, slip, and get up again.

The How-to Steps

So what further steps can you take each day to positively change your belief system and your life?

1) Improve your thought patterns by listening to positive and inspiring audiotapes (see appendix). This will be the best money investment you ever make. Buy several tapes and listen while you are shopping, travelling, walking, doing housework, or whatever. If you take no other advice from this book, this step alone can significantly improve your life.

Alternatively, you can record your own self-tapes, once you understand what works for you. The successful founder of the Celestial Tea Company recorded his own motivation messages and listened every day as he rode his bicycle to work. He started with very little and eventually built a multimillion-dollar company. More importantly, he cherished the pursuit of his dream.

Fill your mind with positive thoughts and beliefs. The best times to listen to such messages are first thing in the morning and last thing at night. Initially, you won't be aware of what is happening, but amazing results will begin to appear. It takes about three months to notice significant change. You will perceive things differently, behave differently and start to see the outcomes you desire.

2) Turn the TV off or be very selective about the kinds of programs you watch and how often you watch. There is nothing inherently bad about TV except that most programs and commercials encourage passive consumption. You cannot create the life you want if you are living through the characters on your television screen.

Evidence also sug-
gests that watching too
much television is
linked to obesity, de-
pression and other
chronic health prob-
lems. A 1993 study pub-

lished in the *Journal of Public Health* found that
24-35% of all commercials are food related. The
greatest concern is the emphasis on high sugar
drinks, snacks and candy. And every time you watch
television you are watching other people earn a great
deal of money. You could be making your own exciting life, instead of watching others live theirs.

3) Evaluate the types of friends you hang out
with. Do they believe in themselves and in you? Are
they helping you to reach your goals or are they the
"misery loves company" type? Choose your friends
carefully and don't spend time with narrow minded
or negative people. Let people know what you need
and how they can be supportive. Ask others what
they need. Without this mutual respect, you may be
forced to end some long-standing relationships.

Even family members can negatively influence
your success. Family members may genuinely want
to help but their fear or limited vision can work
against you. Assess the impact of family members
in the same way you would for a friend. Limit your
exposure to negative people.

Likewise, don't allow so-called "experts" to pull
you down and prevent your success. Experts are

not always right. Know yourself, believe in your goals and ignore the doubters. Listen to people you respect. An excellent way to meet inspiring people and to boost your creative skills is to attend the annual Humor Conference held in New York. For information write to Dr. Joel Goodman at The Humor Conference, Saratoga Springs, New York or visit the internet at *www.humorproject.com.*

4) Decide exactly what you want for your life and set priorities. If you don't know what you want, then start having a good look at what's available. Write out in detail all the things that are important to you. What are your values? What kind of person do you want to become? If you could choose any purpose for your life, what would it be? What *beliefs* do you have to develop to become this kind of person? Be very specific about what you want.

Sperm Bank

Hey lady, you're the one who wanted a movie star with dark hair, strong jaw and deep set eyes (not specific enough).

Write down one or two goals that are currently very important to you. Use Post It™, or similar stickers to pencil in the many steps needed to reach your goals. Arrange your Post Its™ on a big board or wall and move these around as various tasks are completed. Think big when you write your goals. It doesn't matter if they seem to be wild or even impossible. History has shown that great dreamers, who consistently take action, tend to exceed their expectations.

Aim for goals that are meaningful to you and that fill a need. As Robert Schuller says, "The secret of success is simple, find a need and fill it." Past pain may be of help. The pain of bankruptcy may lead to a career in financial counseling. The pain of divorce may lead to writing a book on the topic. Pick worthwhile goals that are meaningful to you, because exclusively materialistic or appearance goals rarely bring long term happiness. Learn more by listening to audiotapes by Les Brown.

5) Visualize the end result and imagine how you will feel when you succeed. Create a *mind's eye view* of your desires. Make the picture vivid, colorful, large and dramatic. You can also add inspiring music.

6) Ask for what you want and need in life. Most people never ask because they are afraid of rejection. If your purpose is sincere and fills a need, then keep asking for assistance. Support will come for worthwhile causes. We must ask ask ask ask ask and then ask again. Adults often stop asking because as children they were told to be quiet.

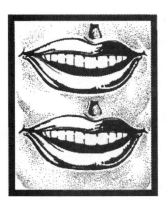

7) Write down and evaluate as many fears as you can think of. Be specific and list those that are

most stopping you from taking action. Pinch your nose and say your fears out loud in an imitation Mickey Mouse voice. This comical voice has a way of making most fears appear ridiculous. A 52-year-old obstetrician once said that this simple technique made him give up medicine and pursue his dream of becoming a commercial photographer.

Think of the downside. What is the worst thing that could happen if you take action? Is your fear reasonable? Do you have a "parachute" to support you if things don't work out? Whenever you feel too afraid to act, consider whether you could survive the worst scenario and if so, just do it. Remember that winners consistently do the things that losers are uncomfortable doing. Start being comfortable by being uncomfortable. Learn more by listening to Louise Hay's audiotape *Overcoming Fears.*

8) Search for and listen to people you respect. Do you know a successful person in your field of work? Have you read their books, listened to their speeches or observed them? Can you ask them for advice? Most successful people have been helped by others and are willing to do the same for you. Ask *enough people* and the relationships you're looking for will appear.

9) Act *as if* you were already the kind of person you want to be. Author and cancer surgeon, Dr. Bernie Siegal, says that if you start acting the way you want to be, you will begin to grow into that type

of person. For example, if you want to be more loving, then start acting more loving. Most of us wait until we get what we think we need to be happy. In fact, we must *first act* the way we want to be and we will then begin to grow into that sort of person.

10) See and think about your problems as opportunities to learn. Embrace problems with a positive, solution focused attitude. Know that all problems can either be solved or managed. Even the ultimate problem of death can be met with peace and serenity. Faith helps us see death as a transition, not an end.

11) Start listening to your internal dialogue. We all say hundreds of things to ourselves each day. Negative thoughts will only change after we become aware of them. Repetitive listening to positive messages can break our negative thought patterns. But practice is essential. Many of my patients have benefited from becoming aware of, and changing, their internal dialogue.

12) If you are unhealthy or overweight or don't have enough money or your relationships aren't working, then feeling upset, angry or guilty will not help you. Start reminding yourself of your good qualities and write these down. Get friends to add to your list and ask them to give you descriptive and specific details of your best qualities. Review these words first thing in the morning and last thing before bed.

13) Patience can be a virtue but the time to start shaping your environment is today. Don't wait for other people, other circumstances or a better time to solve your problems, begin today.

14) Think about what you would be doing if money were not important. If you could choose any purpose in life, what would it be? How can you find the financial means to do what you love? Think about what motivates other people and how you might be mutually supportive.

15) Focus on your dream. The key to success is constancy to purpose. Act with enthusiasm and you will attract others who think in similar ways. At this moment you only know a small percentage of the people who will eventually help you achieve your goals.

16) Nurture curiosity and engage in life long learning. Each moment of your life can be a learning experience and *everyone* you meet has something to teach you. Be open to listening and reap the rewards.

17) Know that difficulties will eventually pass. Master meditator Tich Naht Hagn teaches the reality of life's impermanence. Being aware that nothing stays the same will help us to appreciate present moments. For example, knowing that loved ones will not always be with us can make us value each moment.

18) Stop and take a quiet look at your surroundings. See that almost every object is the result of a human idea. Ideas are everywhere. Your thoughts hold an infinite number of creative possibilities. And money problems are really just idea problems. Money flows to good ideas.

Ideas

19) Adopt an attitude of playfulness. Give yourself permission to be free and playful. Allow for mistakes. Playing the game of life encourages curiosity, creativity and intelligent risk taking.

20) Do not dwell on things you cannot change, such as the personality of others, the system, the administration, politicians, your boss, and so on. Focus on what you can do to change yourself, your thoughts, your actions and your circumstances.

21) List all your successes at the end of the day. Include simple things like drove carefully to work, ate a healthy breakfast, spent time with the kids, finished that report, read that article, etc. Start congratulating yourself and thinking about the things you do well.

22) Greet yourself in the mirror in the same way you would look at your best friend. Use affirming words and review all your positive qualities. Lift your spirits in a way that you would for a loved one. Look

yourself in the eye and hold your gaze with affection and approval. Expect to feel uncomfortable doing this.

23) Choose how to respond to the events in your life. For example, how do you feel if someone calls you a fool? You might think "Oh, that person is right, I'm so stupid, I can't do anything properly." On the other hand, you might think "That person is having a bad day, they're irritable or they have a perceptual handicap and just can't see how wonderful I am." Which way of thinking would bolster your self worth? Eleanor Roosevelt said that no one can make us feel inferior without our consent. We alone are responsible for our feelings.

24) Remind yourself that even the most highly esteemed, wealthy or famous people face numerous difficulties. The tabloids happily reveal that money and fame do not solve problems. Coping successfully means taking a certain perspective on life. We can learn to think in ways that attract joy instead of misery.

25) Turn off the "news." People who have a mindless habit of listening to the news first thing in the morning and again later in the day are programming their mind for negativity. Sure we want to stay informed, but daily radio or television news only highlights tragic events that contribute to fear, inertia and depression. Daily news listening can block both motivation and joy. Replace your news

habit with a few moments of writing in a gratitude journal. Write down several things that you are thankful for.

26) What do you believe is holding you back? Is it really stopping you from pursuing your dreams? Is there anything that is blocking your way? Do you blame your inaction on being too:

- old
- young
- ugly
- short
- tall
- bald
- passive
- foolish
- frail
- fat
- thin
- sick
- weak
- shy
- unlovable
- disabled
- poor
- lonely

History has proven that no matter what your appearance, education, social status, health, race or gender; you can set, pursue and reach worthwhile goals. Danny DeVito is a short, balding movie star. Evelyn Glennie is a completely deaf, yet highly acclaimed musician. Jill Kinmont is a paraplegic high school teacher. Mother Teresa became world famous and worked well into her 80's. Oprah Winfrey was an overweight black woman who built a media empire. Rocha Iglesias is an 86-year-old masters level track star. Terry Fox ran across Canada with one leg. The list goes on and on.

Do not fool yourself by saying that these people were or are simply more courageous or different than you. The same spirit is within each one of us. We need only *begin* to develop it. The people just listed were not all born better looking or richer or slimmer or smarter. Life did not present them with every opportunity. They succeeded by developing their thoughts and beliefs and by taking persistent action.

Are your thoughts and beliefs concerning food and lifestyle producing the outcomes you desire?

Do you hold any of these beliefs?

- I can't eat breakfast.
- I must have my coffee.
- I can't cook.
- I hate vegetables.
- I dislike mornings.
- I must watch TV.
- I'm not humorous.
- People dislike me.
- I must eat bread.
- It's too difficult.
- I dislike exercising.
- I can't get healthy.
- I've tried everything.
- I dislike being alone.
- I need chocolate.

- I can't change.
- It's not my fault.
- I have to work then.
- I'm too old to bike.
- That's just my fate.
- Others are to blame.
- I'm getting too old.
- My kids are to blame.
- My spouse is to blame.
- I can't lift weights.
- It's too expensive.
- Doctors will cure me.
- It's too risky.

Do you hold any of the previous beliefs in your subconscious mind? You can probably add even more statements to the list. Look carefully at any statement that you think is true. These beliefs become self-fulfilling and are deeply imbedded in our character. But with time and practice, you can discard them. To paraphrase from a great book: you will discover the truth and the truth will set you free.

The first step toward conscious living is knowing that the majority of your negative beliefs can be changed. Remember that your current beliefs have formed over many years and it takes time to imprint your mind with more useful messages. Like a child who lives down to being told hundreds of times that she is "careless" or "sloppy" or "lazy," our new conditioning must also involve *long term, positive and persistent repetition.* Feed your need and you will succeed.

This chapter has revealed several different ways to reprogram your thoughts. It bears repeating that one of the simplest methods is to listen to positive and inspiring audiotapes. Within three months of doing this *every day,* you will begin to see dramatic changes.

Then celebrate, for ...

...wisdom, grace and kindness and the power of your love will be, a measure of the legacy you leave.

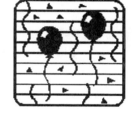

David Roth

10.

Top Ten Tips

News and Reviews

This chapter will review and present further details for making the most of your new lifestyle. Attending to many small details will create remarkable results. Give yourself plenty of time to learn, experiment with, and adopt new hab-

its. As well, *give your new habits time to work*. Believe in and visualize the outcome you desire.

1. Drink sufficient water.

Drink *at least* one large glass of water or carbohydrate free drink about one-half hour before each meal or snack. Consume *at least* six (8 fl. oz.), preferably more, glasses of water daily.

Over 70 percent of the human body is made up of water. We can live longer without food than without water. Adequate water is also required to metabolize protein. It is important to *think* about drinking water because most people rarely feel thirsty. Dehydration is a common problem, especially among the elderly.

Think to drink ... enough water.

Go into any acute care hospital and you will see most of the patients attached to intravenous lines connected to bags of (mainly) *water!* The number of health disorders related to low water intake, and helped by re-hydration, is remarkable. Ask any medical-surgical nurse how many patients are admitted with the diagnosis of dehydration and you will begin to understand the importance of drinking water. Furthermore, dehydration may not be listed as the main diagnosis but as an indirect cause of the condition (for example, urinary tract infections).

Most of us know that we need to consume plenty of water but *doing so* is not always easy. If remembering is a problem, then devise a memory jogger such as setting your watch alarm or putting notes where you will see them or carrying a daily water bottle. Do whatever works for you. One of my patients puts water into a 2-liter bottle every morning, as a reminder to drink at least this much by the end of the day.

There are several ways of consuming enough water but drinking lots of caffeine (coffee, tea, etc.) is not the solution. Caffeine increases insulin levels and excess quantities are associated with a variety of health problems, especially for menopausal women.

Sweet drinks such as soft drinks and fruit or even vegetable juice increase insulin levels, promote fat storage and do not improve hydration. In fact, sugar loaded drinks draw water out of body cells. Read labels and use products that contain zero, that is, *no* carbohydrate.

And while there are several no carbohydrate drink alternatives, we recommend that you try drinking just plain water. Your taste buds may be conditioned to enjoy various sensations, but they can be retrained. Continually stimulating your palette with overly sweet or strong tasting foods usually creates a continuing desire for more food.

Your taste preferences have been learned. For example, a child raised in the traditional English culture is more likely to enjoy sweets than a child raised in Japan. People who have moved between cultures know that humans are not passive victims of conditioning. Given time and willingness, we can adapt to and enjoy a wide variety of tastes.

Some people dislike drinking plain water, but imagine for a moment that you are stranded in the middle of a hot desert. That simple glass of icy water will start to look very appealing. Still not convinced? Then try adding a little decaffeinated green tea, lemon, ice and stevia for a refreshing and healthy way to hydrate your body. Green tea also contains antioxidants that can help slow aging.

Green
Tea

Finally, you may want to think about drinking a reasonable portion of your water early in the day. This can improve your chances for an uninterrupted sleep, especially for older adults. Avoiding fluids after a certain time, for example 7 P.M., will help prevent bladder related sleep disturbance.

2. Regularly consume soy foods as part of your protein intake.

Add some form of soy protein such as tofu, soy flour or soy imitation meats to your daily, or at least weekly, menu. Soy foods such as tofu are an important part of a healthy diet. Firm tofu is preferred since it is more protein dense than the soft varieties. Getting adequate protein from soft tofu would require you to eat large amounts of this product.

There is good evidence to suggest that soybean products can help decrease the risk of cancer, osteoporosis and even heart disease. Menopausal women also benefit from the natural estrogens found in soy foods.

3. Regularly consume fibrous vegetables.

Look at examples of fibrous vegetables in the food column list (chapter seven). These include such things as asparagus, lettuce, green beans, broccoli, cauliflower and many more. Eat a variety of fibrous vegetables at lunch or dinner. Frozen vegetables are especially quick and convenient and can retain even *more vitamins* than long stored "fresh" vegetables.

Simply pop a serving of single or mixed frozen vegetables in the microwave, add a bit of grated cheese, olive oil, spices, soy sauce or other flavorings and you have a delicious, filling and nutritious side dish. Blending tofu and mixed spices into a creamy and satisfying dip can also enhance the flavor of raw vegetables.

Fibrous vegetables contain relatively small amounts of carbohydrate. Most vegetables also have a low sugar speed, which means that their carbohydrate is turned into blood glucose very *slowly*.

Fibrous vegetables are also high in water, bulk and the fiber that help to limit constipation. In addition, mixed vegetables optimize your intake of vitamins and minerals. Remember, however, that fibrous vegetables *do not* include such things as potatoes, corn, baked beans, yams, beets, carrots, kidney beans and other starchy vegetables.

Vegetables contain dozens of phytochemicals such as indoles, lignans and flavanoids which contribute to good health. For example, cruciferous vegetables such as broccoli and brussel sprouts contain well-known anti-cancer agents. Scientific study of these nutrients is in its infancy and each day there are new substances being identified and tested.

4. Include omega 3 fat sources.

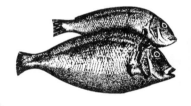

Consume at least two servings per week of salmon, mackerel or sardines. Tuna, sole and other fish are also good choices, but contain lower amounts of omega-3 fat. Alternatively, you may use 1-2 teaspoons per day of cod liver oil, which is available in pleasant tasting flavors.

Dozens of well designed research studies support the benefits of fish fat. (See chapter six and seven.)

5. Add mono-unsaturated fat.

Add a small amount of mono-unsaturated fat such as olive oil, almonds or avocado (others in food column list, chapter seven) to meals and snacks.

Fat is hormonally neutral and will not raise insulin levels. When fat is mixed with food it also acts to slow the absorption of carbohydrate into the blood stream. Mono-unsaturated fat improves the taste of food and causes the release of a satisfaction hormone known as cholecystokinin (CCK).

Certain high fat foods such as avocados (or mashed as guacamole) and nuts also contain magnesium, which plays a vital role in nerve and muscle functioning. It also prevents constipation.

Avocados: rich in nutrients and good fat.

Nuts contain reasonable amounts of zinc, which acts to strengthen the immune system. Zinc lozenges, for example, have been shown to decrease the length and severity of cold viruses.

6. *Eat smaller meals and snacks more frequently.*

Prevent excess hunger by never allowing more than five hours to go by without eating a small snack or meal. If overeating is a problem, then try eating the right mix and amount of food every 3–4 hours.

Plan to eat a protein rich breakfast within one hour of waking up. The ideal meal pattern for an active adult is three small meals a day plus a mid morning, mid afternoon and light evening snack. Choose what works for you and write it down.

About 75% of my overweight or chronically ill patients initially display what has been called the "starve and stuff syndrome." An extreme example is the person who goes all day without eating and then consumes large amounts in the evening. Other variations include people who eat one or two large meals a day, yet continue to feel lethargic and gain weight. They commonly avoid eating breakfast.

The physiological and psychological dynamics of this behavior are complex. People tell me they don't feel hungry in the morning, or they are too busy to have breakfast or when they eat breakfast they feel too hungry later on. Breaking this negative cycle involves changing entire life patterns. Fatigue, late nights, emotional disturbances, poor nutrition, lack of exercise and *irregular routines* are all interconnected.

Remember that the best time to eat is when you are not overly hungry. Excess hunger is a sign that blood sugar has dropped too low. People then eat too much food in the time it takes their brain to register normal blood sugar levels.

It is also wise to be aware of your behavior when eating in social situations. People tend to eat more food in the company of others. For example, a 1992 study published in the journal *Physiology and Behavior* found that meals eaten in large groups were over 75% larger than when eaten alone. This doesn't mean it is better to avoid socializing, simply be aware of your eating.

7. *Write down some* realistic *activity goals.*

Think about your current *lifestyle* and how much activity you do. Getting enough exercise can, but does not necessarily mean, joining a health club or buying exercise equipment. The key is *consistency of habit.* We need small and realistic goals that can be comfortably continued into old age. Ask yourself "could I still do this exercise routine at the age of 70?"

Anyone who says there is no time to fit activity into their lifestyle is not serious about wanting greater health and energy. As a popular dental office sign says "ignore your teeth, they'll go away." Ignore regular activity and your health will also go away.

Ignore your teeth, they'll go away.

8. *Stay motivated by reading and acting on suggestions in chapter nine.*

Information alone is not enough to make people take appropriate action. Most adults know they should exercise, get enough sleep, eat properly, drink water, not smoke and so on. We know what to do, but even health professionals may not do it. The key lies in our subconscious conditioning and a realization that this can be changed.

Remember the lessons from advertising. Advertisers pay millions of dollars for television and other media promotions because they know it works. Advertising affects our subconscious mind and makes even intelligent people buy things they don't really need. Miraculous change occurs when we begin to understand how to program our subconscious.

It is also important to remember that at any moment in time, you have the power to figuratively reach within your mind and create the biochemistry of calm and peace. Getting in touch with this state enables us to react to any situation in the best possible light. It promotes clarity of thought and helps us choose a response that leads to favorable outcomes.

Do you doubt the ability of *chosen thoughts* to create a chemical change in your body? Just think of cutting into a tart lemon and imagine passing your tongue over the clear juice. Your mind has caused your mouth to water. This chemical change is merely a reaction to the thoughts that *you alone* have chosen.

Similarly, we can produce favorable body chemistry by mindfully recapturing good feelings from our past. Remember a moment when you felt completely at ease or blissfully happy, and now recall, in great detail, the sights, sounds and smells of this moment. This was a time of serenity or joy and there was no stress response to bring on the release of potentially harmful hormones such as cortisol, adrenaline or excess insulin.

Some longevity researchers even believe that the physical changes of aging are caused by an accumulation of painful or sad memories stored in our subconscious. Year after year these negative memories are reviewed and the physical results are created over and over again.

It makes sense that if we could consistently use our mind to create a favorable body chemistry then we would at least slow the aging process. Indeed, one of the key features of those who live exceptionally long lives is that they tend to be psychologically unflappable. That is, not much seems to bother them. Choose your thoughts, and to some extent, your body will change.

9. Think and Plan

Any success requires that we think and plan ahead of time. People often say they have no time, but if there's time for television, complaining or sleeping too much, then there's time to plan our food strategy. Here are some time saving tips for busy people:

Keep your freezer well stocked with several varieties of frozen fruits and vegetables. Use a microwave oven to easily prepare just the desired amount. Remember that frozen foods can be even more vitamin-rich than fresh items. Canned fruits and vegetables are also quick and handy. Add them to fresh or frozen varieties. Another time saver is to prepare large portions of fresh fruit or veggies and keep them refrigerated. This is easier than daily chopping of fresh produce.

Use lime or lemon juice over large bowls of fruit to keep them from turning brown. For a sweeter taste, sprinkle a bit of stevia (a sweetener found in most health food stores) over the top. Mix well. Try to vary your fruit mixtures by adding items of different colors and textures. Frozen blueberries or raspberries add a pleasant touch to a mixed fruit salad.

Salad greens and dressings — Wash and prepare a large amount of salad fixings all at once and keep in refrigerator bags or covered bowls for quick side dishes. Or, if you don't mind the expense, buy the pre-washed varieties. Add some black olives, peppers or tomatoes. Use creamy low or no carbohydrate dressings.

Quick Protein Sources

It is typically easy to find carbohydrate snacks, but quick protein takes a bit more planning. Make sure your fridge is well stocked with a variety of easy and tasty protein portions. You could try:

- string cheese

- individually wrapped cheese slices

- cream cheese or silken tofu — mix with spices like onion, garlic, or herbs as desired and use as a vegetable dip

- protein powder to mix with yogurt, oatmeal, milk or other foods

- sliced turkey, chicken, ham, or other lean meats

- boiled eggs — boil several at a time and re-frigerate

- cottage cheese — great with fruit

- soy burgers, dogs, slices — freeze or refrigerate

- fish cakes — use large cans of salmon, tuna, mackerel or other fish and prepare four or five fish cakes in advance (visit our website for recipes at www.feedyourneeds.com)

- brewer's yeast can be a quick and nutritious protein addition to yogurt, oatmeal or other foods—add stevia or fruit for better taste

- blend some fruit with ricotta cheese and stevia, then freeze for a quick and delicious dessert

- prepare and freeze a batch of protein muffins or oatmeal bars (see website recipes). Grab and bag one for an afternoon snack

- if you're really pressed for time you could use one of the commercial snack bars that have a 40-30-30 ratio of carbohydrate, fat and pro-tein (e.g., Zone™ or Balance Bars™)

Quick, No Cook GLA

Have you no time or patience to cook oatmeal? Then try using another form of oats. Grind a large batch of whole or steel cut oats in an electric coffee grinder (whole oats look a bit like rice). Keep a large container of ground oats on hand and add a spoon or two to yogurt or other foods. It will provide you with gamma linoleic acid (GLA) and a good source of soluble fiber.

Crunch and Chew Factors

Low carbohydrate eating need not be low on crunch. Here are some easy solutions:

Crunch Choices

- popcorn with grated parmesan cheese

- baked egg whites — add stevia or other flavorings

- low carbohydrate crackers such as bran crispbread, rye crispbreads etc (read labels for carbo content)

- raw or roasted nuts or seeds

- chopped celery — great to mix with tuna or other fish.

- raw carrots, zucchini, celery and other vegetables — keep crisp in water. Add creamy cheese or meat spreads

Chewing Gum

Do you still feel an urge to chew? Psychiatrists have found that the human brain produces a feel good chemical called serotonin, simply from repeated jaw motion. You may wish to try sugarless chewing gum, but remember that one stick of sugarless gum still contains anywhere from 1 to 7 grams of carbohydrate.

Chewing gum can also help those with delayed stomach emptying, especially people with diabetes. Chewing stimulates the release of enzyme rich saliva. It also increases muscular activity in your stomach. Chewing a small amount of gum for an hour or so after a meal will aid digestion. It is unwise, however, to adopt a chronic gum chewing habit. Mindless chewing, especially with a loud or open-mouthed nature is offensive.

10. The Cost Factor

Our food suggestions may be less expensive than your previous eating style, especially if past hunger made you buy lots of packaged junk food. On the other hand, eating high quality protein, fruits, nuts and vegetables will cost you more than bread, bagels or pasta.

Some people complain about the cost of eating well, yet focussing your saving efforts on food is a bad investment. How costly is it to feel chronically sick or tired? What good is saving for your retirement if you don't live to see it? In fact, a high percentage of people die within the first two years of retirement. Family members then inherit your money and go on a luxury vacation. Good thing you saved on food.

How much do you spend on your car, cable TV, home improvements, vacations or other entertainment? Spending money to preserve and repair your body is the foundation for enjoying life. Lose health and you lose everything. All this being said, if you are still interested in trying to spend less on food, here are some suggestions:

- make yogurt from bulk milk powder
- make soymilk or tofu — see appendix
- buy bulk protein powders
- buy bulk canned goods
- stew cheaper, less tender cuts of meat
- discover where local fruit and vegetable markets buy their produce and shop there
- use mackerel or sardines, instead of salmon or other more costly fish
- quick freeze (may need to blanch) seasonal fruits and vegetables in portion packs
- split the cost of bulk buy foods with friends
- freeze portions of bulk meat, poultry, fish
- pick and preserve your own fresh produce
- watch for store specials, stock up, or join co-ops

11.

Appendix: Lists and Resources

Sugar Speed of Common Foods

The following is a list of common foods, organized according to their sugar speed (glycemic index).

Fruits —

Better choices:
(low speed sugar)
plums
pears
cherries
nectarines
apples
grapefruit
blueberries
apricots (fresh)
raspberries

grapes
peaches
avocado (use for fat)
orange

Poorer Choices:
(use as condiments)

papaya
mango
raisins
banana
watermelon

205

Vegetables —

Better Choices:
(low speed sugar)
asparagus
broccoli
brussel sprouts
eggplant
onions
mushrooms
string beans
zucchini
cabbage
sauerkraut
cauliflower
spinach
peppers
celery
lettuce
radishes

Poorer Choices:
(use as condiments)
pumpkin
green peas
sweet corn
baked beans

Grain Based Foods —

Better Choices:
barley
oats (whole or steel cut)
rolled oats (slow cooking)
oat bran bread
rye kernel bread
mixed whole grain loaf
pumpernickel
bulger bread
plain bran
rice bran
bulgar
brown rice
basmati rice
rye

Poorer Choices:
Anything made with wheat, including flour and white bread, white or light brown bagels, bread stuffing, kaiser rolls, gluten free wheat bread, French baguettes, etc.

white rice
converted rice
corn flakes
rice crisps
tapioca
vanilla wafers
rice cakes
most cookies
puffed crispbread

Legumes —

(high in
  carbohydrate,
  use only small
  amounts)

Better Choices:
black eyed beans
butter beans
chick peas
kidney beans
red or green lentils
lima beans
soy beans
pinto beans
navy beans

Poorer Choices:
(Use as condiments)
baked beans
broad beans
fava beans
canned kidney beans
canned lentils
yellow split peas
Root vegetables

Better Choices
(use only small
  amounts)
red potato
new white potato
yams

Poorer Choices:
(high sugar speed)
parsnips
carrots
instant potato
baked potato
mashed potato
French fries
microwaved potato
rutabaga

Sweeteners —

Better Choices:
Stevia herb (no carbs
  or calories)
Equal or other no
  calorie sweetener
Fructose (contains
  carbohydrate: use
  only small amounts)

Poorer Choices:
maltose
glucose
honey
white or brown sugar
syrups

Miscellaneous —
(Low Sugar Speed)
peanuts
almonds
brazil nuts

Your Food Chart

Most people like to eat the same 20 to 30 different foods over and over again. The chart on the next page can help you understand more about the foods that you eat on a regular basis. Add two more columns for protein and fat if you want further information.

Use any good food count book to look up these values, such as. *The Complete Book of Food Counts* by Corinne T. Netzer.

And remember that you can still use the simple eyeball method.

Know Your Foods

Your Name _____

Foods Eaten Often	Usual Size	Carbo Grams
_____	_____	_____
_____	_____	_____
_____	_____	_____
_____	_____	_____
_____	_____	_____
_____	_____	_____
_____	_____	_____
_____	_____	_____
_____	_____	_____
_____	_____	_____
_____	_____	_____
_____	_____	_____
_____	_____	_____
_____	_____	_____
_____	_____	_____

Resources

1. Useful low or no carb products:

Scandinavian Bran Crispbread: originates in Norway but distributed by Cel-Ent, Inc., Box 1173, Beaufort, SC 29901. There are only 2 grams of carbohydrate in each slice.

Bran-a Crisp: originates in Norway but available from Interbrands, Inc., 3300 N.E. 164th St., FF3, Ridgefield, WA 98642. There are only 3 grams of carbohydrate in each slice.

Phone orders for both crisp breads are available by calling toll free: (800) 735-7726

Toasted Nori : A very tasty low carbohydrate snack available through many health food stores. It includes a unique mixture of barley, soybeans, rice, red pepper and a special type of seaweed.

A typical strip contains only 0.12 grams of carbohydrate, but brands vary, so read the label.

Stevia: a safe and natural herb sweetener that contains no carbohydrate. The plant has been used for hundreds of years in Asia, but in 1931 two French chemists, Bridel and Lavielle, refined the extraction process. Stevia now comes in a white powder or liquid form. It can be used in cooking and is about 300 times sweeter than table sugar. Look for it in health food stores.

No-Cal Brand Syrups — Sold in many supermarkets and also distributed by H. Fox and Co., Inc., Brooklyn, NY 11212. These no calorie, no carbohydrate flavorings may be used in hot drinks, desserts, on fruit, even over tofu or eggs. More suggestions available from the distributor.

Soymilk makers can be purchased from Alternative Solutions, 5 Sagebrush Lane, Don Mills, Ontario. Call (416) 391-4831.

Fish oil supplements — There are different kinds of fish oil supplements. A pleasant tasting one is an emulsified variety made by Twin Lab and called "Dale Alexander's Fish Oil Concentrate." It is widely available. Their address is Ronkonkoma, New York, 11779 U.S.A.

Vegetarian Protein — A variety of superb soy "meat" products are available in many grocery stores. If you cannot locate what you want, contact **Yves Veggie Cuisine**, 1638 Derwent Way, Delta (Vancouver), B.C. V3M 6R9. You can also email them at *yvc@yvesveggie.com*

2. *Mind and Life Changing Audiotapes*

(guaranteed to improve "act-itude" / motivation)

Dare to Win — Canfield and Hansen
Live Your Dreams — Les Brown

Life Leaves Clues — Corinne Peachment
Power Thoughts — Dr. Robert Schuller
Overcoming Fears — Dr. Louise Hay
Art of Mindful Living — Thich Nhat Hanh
Revolution from Within — Gloria Steinem
Power of the Mind to Heal — Dr. Joan Borysenko
Timeless Healing — Dr. Herbert Benson
Be Happy — Richard Carlson

3. Looking for Recipes?

This book was written and designed to help people *understand* how food affects hormones and health and to provide readers with practical techniques for boosting motivation. It is not meant to encourage "dieting" or following any specific group of recipes.

Long term dieting, or adhering to what others want you to eat rarely works because each of us has different food preferences. We gain health when we begin to understand food and discover how to balance the fat, protein and carbohydrate that is contained in what we like to eat.

All this being said, if you are still interested in specific recipes or would like further resources to help you reach your goals, they can be found, free of charge, by visiting our web site at **www.feedyourneeds.com** (remember the "s").

Alternatively, there are several books that will provide appropriate recipes. These include:

1) *Protein Power* by husband and wife physicians, Michael Eades and Mary Dan Eades.

2) *Zone Meals in Minutes* by Dr. Barry Sears

3) *Carbohydrate Addicts' Diet* by Dr. R. Heller

4) *Your Fat is Not Your Fault* by Carol Simontacchi

References

Over 100 scientific references to support the information presented in this book can be found free of charge by visiting our website at:

www.feedyourneeds.com
(Remember the "s")

12.

Index

Feed Your Need

Someone you know would benefit from reading *Feed Your Need*. It's the ideal gift for anyone you care about—easy to understand, enjoyable and life changing.

Please rush _____ copies of **Feed Your Need** to me. Each copy is $14.95 and this includes shipping and handling. Enclosed is a check for $ _____ (U.S.) made payable to Marpel.

Full Name: _____

Address: _____

City: _____

State or Province: _____

Postal Code: _____

Telephone or email: _____

*Discounts are offered for purchasing 10 or more books.
Author Corinne Peachment is also available
to entertain and educate your group.
Email or write for details.*

MARPEL

P. O. Box 8478
Austin, Tx, 78713-8478, U.S.A
Email: foodgame@earthlink.net
www.feedyourneeds.com

Please allow 4-6 weeks for delivery.